THE PASTRY SCHOOL

THE PASTRY SCHOOL

Sweet and Savoury Pies, Tarts and Treats to Bake at Home

Julie Jones

PHOTOGRAPHY BY PETER CASSIDY

KYLE BOOKS

For my Mum,

In memory of an incredible bond and love we shared.
You will forever be with me when I'm baking.

Love you so much, Julie x

An Hachette UK Company
www.hachette.co.uk

First published in Great Britain in 2020 by
Kyle Books, an imprint of Kyle Cathie Ltd
Carmelite House
50 Victoria Embankment
London EC4Y 0DZ
www.kylebooks.co.uk

ISBN: 978 0 85783 7806

Distributed in the US by Hachette Book Group,
1290 Avenue of the Americas, 4th and 5th Floors,
New York, NY 10104

Distributed in Canada by Canadian Manda Group,
664 Annette St., Toronto, Ontario, Canada M6S 2C8

Publisher: Joanna Copestick
Editor: Isabel Gonzalez-Prendergast
Design: Rachel Cross
Photography: Peter Cassidy
Food styling: Julie Jones
Props styling: Cynthia Blackett
Production: Gemma John and Nic Jones

A Cataloguing in Publication record for this title is
available from the British Library

Printed and bound in China

10 9 8 7 6 5 4 3 2 1

A FEW NOTES:

Please note all spoons are level, and when a recipe calls for eggs, medium are used.

Where grams have been converted to ounces and cups: please note that all recipes were written and tested using grams, therefore I would suggest using this measurement system, if possible.

All recipes were tested in a fan oven at the temperatures stated.

Unfortunately I haven't yet found a good plastic-free alternative to cling film, though I am still searching.

Contents

A pastry revival is taking the world by storm – and I am excited by it. With top restaurants once again featuring pies and pithiviers on their menus; artisan bakeries opening up aplenty; and Instagram awash with pie-art and viennoiserie, it is safe to say that pastry of all varieties is firmly back in vogue.

Let's not get confused here, there's pastry and then there's pastry. The first is pale, mass-produced, tasteless, and often wrapped around a questionable filling. The second is hand-crafted, beautifully made and golden, delivering both excellent texture and depth of flavour. These pastries are quite simply incomparable – lovingly-made pastry is the starring role of a dish, not merely a vehicle to carry its contents.

As many will know, being creative with pastry is my favourite pastime. The hours I have spent honing my skills have been the most peaceful of my life. I find the whole process soothing; those mindful hours spent making pies have given both clarity of mind and a renewed sense of creativity. Artistry aside, what we mustn't forget is that the fundamental, most important and rewarding aspect of making and baking with pastry should always be in the eating. I have many food memories, yet it is those that are enveloped in pastry that are the most memorable. My Nana Maud's custard tart, mince pies at Christmas, an unctuous oxtail pie and Sfogliatella, to name just a few. Although all are very different, I fondly remember each because of the pastry; crisp, golden and flaking, just as it should be. Would they be as memorable if they had been under-baked, flabby and disappointing? Definitely not.

I often hear that reoccurring disappointments during baking not only dishearten but completely deter even the most experienced home baker from making pastry again. Upon questioning, this is mostly due to the cause of disappointment remaining a mystery. With the problem unresolved, subsequent attempts will remain just as, if not more, disheartening than the first. It is therefore understandable that many surrender to the convenience of a shop-bought, ready-made alternative.

Pastry, it seems, is the nemesis of many. I really want to change that. With this in mind, my aim in writing this book was to eliminate these shortcomings from the outset, to ensure that making and baking with pastry would be a pleasurable, peaceful and successful experience for all. How? By simplifying each process and cutting out the jargon, creating easy-to-follow, failsafe recipes that require neither expensive or professional equipment, nor a degree in patisserie.

Believe me when I say that I have willingly encountered every problem possible during testing, so that you don't have to. I have seen the buttery layers between puff pastry rupture and choux buns deflate, crack and wither before my eyes. My inverted puff pastry has misbehaved in all ways imaginable and I have had more tears in my sheet pastry than a colander has holes. Yet with contemplation, investigation, patience and perseverance, I believe that I have pinpointed and eliminated the possible cause of each. Patience; try to skip a step or save a few minutes here and there, rush any stage of making – right through to baking – and the pastry will undoubtedly suffer for it and ultimately time will be wasted.

Over the next few pages there are recipes for many different pastries – 10 in total. From shortcrust to sheet, vegan to viennoiserie; and dare I be boastful in declaring that I have included a tasty, crunchy, easy-to-roll, gluten-free recipe, too? The recipe chapters that follow give plenty of inspiration for how to use each of these pastries, both savoury and sweet – some are traditional, some inventive, all delicious. Within each recipe and on pages 44–45 you will find a key, a recommendation of the other pastries that could be used as an alternative to the one featured, proving pastry to be a most versatile component.

My hope is that this book will bring confidence and success to your baking and that you will embrace pastry-making with vigour, and, when a recipe calls for it, be inclined to make your own every time, so that using shop-bought pastry becomes a thing of the past.

Hone your skills and pass them down, keep the revival going, and never forget to share the undoubted knowledge that...

'Patience with pastry is key!'

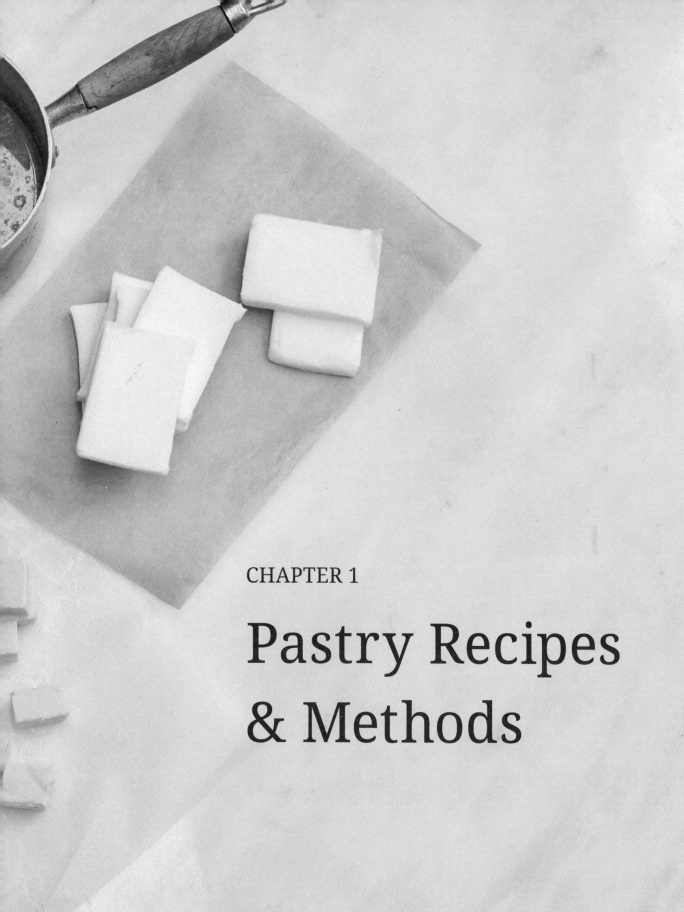

CHAPTER 1

Pastry Recipes & Methods

SALTED SHORTCRUST PASTRY

This is a great pastry – crumbly, tasty and crisp, perfect for encasing savoury fillings. The secret is in baking it longer than you would imagine to be necessary. There is no joy in eating flabby pastry, and definitely no appeal in that soggy bottom! This recipe yields enough to line a large circular tin measuring 23 x 3.5cm (9 x 1½in), with some left over for small decorations. If you are making a covered pie, you will need to make a double quantity.

MAKES 1 QUANTITY

230g (8oz/1¾ cups) plain (all-purpose) flour
125g (4½oz/½ cup plus 1 tablespoon) cold unsalted butter, cut into 1cm (½in) cubes, no need to be precise
1 teaspoon fine salt
1 egg yolk
2 tablespoons milk

For egg wash – if and when the recipe calls for it
1 egg yolk
boiling water

In the bowl of a freestanding mixer, place the flour, butter and salt **(1)**. Attach the paddle and mix on a medium speed until the butter has been incorporated into the flour and resembles fine breadcrumbs. Add the egg yolk and milk **(2)** and continue to mix, switching off the mixer the very moment a cohesive dough forms **(3)** – this should only take 30–60 seconds, depending on your mixer. Turn out the pastry onto a work surface – there's no need for more flour – and bring swiftly together with your hands without overworking **(4)**.

Lay out a long sheet of cling film and place the dough on one half. Flatten the pastry with the palms of your hands, then fold the remaining cling film over the top, fully encasing the dough. Roll out between the cling film to an approximate depth of 5mm (¼in), trying to keep it in a circular shape **(5)**. If using to decorate a pie top, rest in the fridge for at least an hour. If using to line a pastry case, I have found that chilling this salted shortcrust prior to doing so will result in the pastry cracking when it is folded into the tin's edge. If you are lining a pastry case, after rolling between the cling film, rest the pastry outside of the fridge in a relatively cool place for at least an hour.

After resting, roll out the pastry between two sheets of non-stick baking paper **(6)** – there is no need for extra flour. The pastry is now ready for use, whether topping a pie or lining a tin. Please note that an unbaked pastry case will require chilling in the fridge for at least 30 minutes prior to baking.

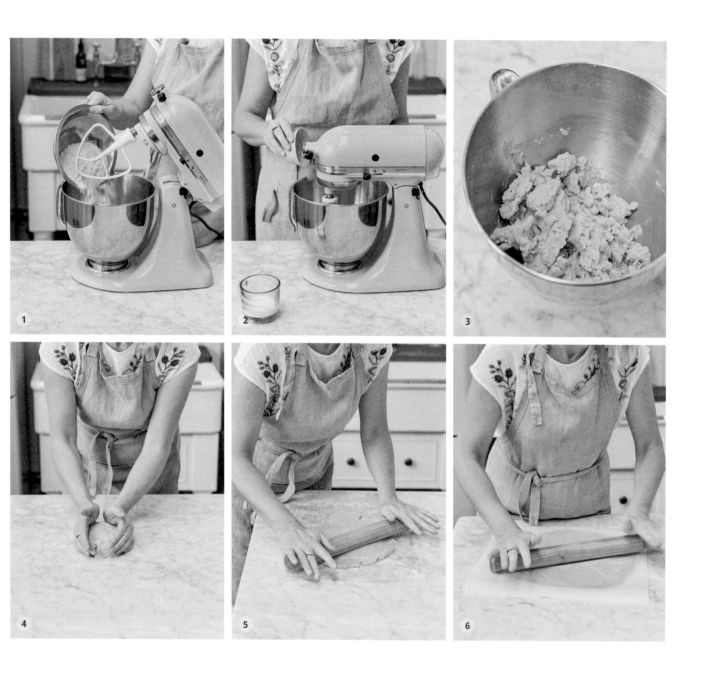

For tips on successfully lining tins, blind baking and trimming a pastry case, see page 38.

SWEET SHORTCRUST PASTRY

This classic pastry is my go-to recipe for most of the sweet pies and tarts in this book. No alterations are needed from one recipe to the next, other than the quantity needed. That said, if you are feeling experimental, additional flavourings such as citrus zest, vanilla, ground nuts and spices can be added successfully, although do use them sparingly. To overpower the perfect buttery taste that this pastry offers would be a great shame. Personally, I prefer to focus the layering of flavour into the pie or tart filling instead.

One quantity of pastry is enough to line a large circular tin measuring 23 x 3.5cm (9 x 1½in), with extra remaining for small decorations. For a fully covered decorative pie, a double quantity will be needed.

MAKES 1 QUANTITY

230g (8oz/1¾ cups) plain (all-purpose) flour
125g (4½oz/½ cup plus 1 tablespoon) cold
   unsalted butter, cut into 1cm (½in) cubes,
   no need to be precise
50g (1¾oz/heaping ⅓ cup) icing (powdered)
   sugar
1 egg yolk
2 tablespoons milk

**For egg wash – if and when the recipe
   calls for it**
1 egg yolk
boiling water

Place the flour and butter into the bowl of a freestanding mixer and attach the paddle beater. Mix on a medium speed until the butter has been incorporated into the flour and resembles fine breadcrumbs **(1)**. Add the icing (powdered) sugar and mix for a few seconds before adding the egg yolk and milk **(2)**. Continue to mix until a cohesive dough forms **(3)** – this should only take 30–60 seconds, depending on your mixer. Turn out the pastry onto a work surface – there's no need for more flour – and bring it swiftly together with your hands, without overworking it **(4)**.

Lay out a long sheet of cling film and place the dough on one half. Flatten the pastry with the palms of your hands, then fold the remaining cling film over the top, fully encasing the dough. Roll out swiftly between the cling film **(5)** to an approximate depth of 5mm (¼in), trying your best to keep it in a circular shape. Place in the fridge for at least an hour before using.

After resting, roll out between two sheets of non-stick baking paper **(6)** – there's no need for more flour – and use according to the relevant recipe instructions.

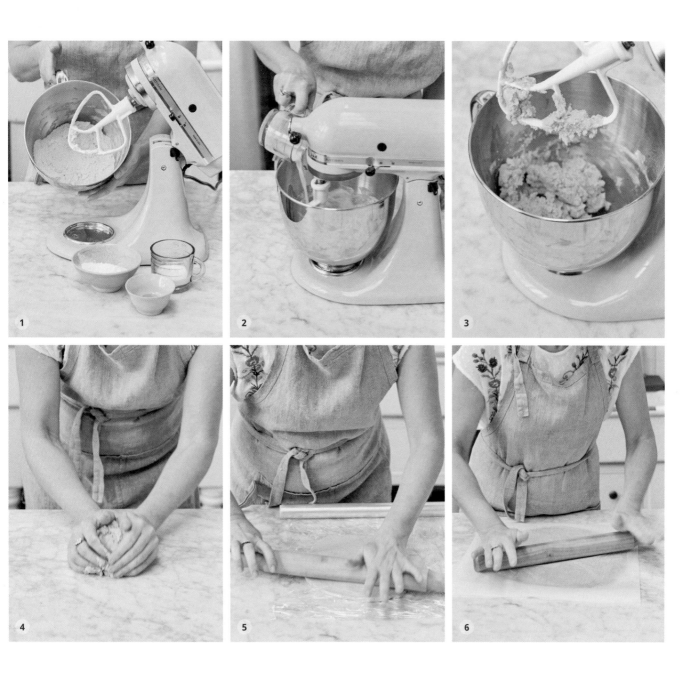

For tips on successfully lining tins, blind baking and trimming a pastry case, see page 38.

HOT WATER PASTRY

This tasty pastry has great flavour as well as texture, and the beautiful, deep golden colour when baked is so appealing. Although traditionally used for encasing meat pies that are served cold, this pastry works successfully with many other fillings, too, and is equally as delicious (if not better, in my opinion) served warm. It really is easy to make and great to work with, due to its pliability – it won't crack or break when lining tins, and thin strips of pastry can be rolled to surprising lengths which can then be plaited and used to create many a decorative finish.

Contrary to popular belief, this pastry can be rolled out and used when cold, the name confusing many into thinking it must be used when hot. This recipe makes enough pastry for a large pie with a little extra for décor; if a smaller amount is needed, a half quantity can be made – to halve the egg, simply beat, weigh, then halve it accordingly, before adding to the flour.

MAKES 1 QUANTITY

450g (1lb/scant 3½ cups) plain (all-purpose) flour, plus extra for dusting
1½ teaspoons fine salt
1 egg
175ml (6fl oz/¾ cup) cold water
100g (3½oz/½ cup minus 1 tablespoon) unsalted butter, cut into 1cm (½in) cubes, no need to be precise
75g (2⅔oz/⅓ cup) lard, cut into 1cm (½in) cubes, no need to be precise

For egg wash – if and when the recipe calls for it
1 egg yolk
boiling water

Place the flour and salt in a large bowl and briefly mix to combine. Make a well in the centre of the flour, crack in the egg and mix through with a fork **(1)**. Gently heat the water, butter and lard in a small saucepan **(2)** until the fats have melted. Increase the heat and allow the water to boil for 20 seconds or so, then remove from the heat.

Using a slow yet steady stream, pour the liquid into the flour **(3)**, mixing with a spatula or wooden spoon to form a thick paste **(4)**. Give the paste a quick but vigorous mix, then cover the bowl with a damp cloth **(5)** and leave to rest at room temperature for 1 hour.

Turn out onto a lightly floured work surface and knead with your hands for about 30 seconds, until the dough looks smoother, paler and more pastry like **(6)**. Wrap in cling film and place in the fridge for a minimum of 30 minutes, preferably no longer than 1 hour.

Roll out onto a lightly floured surface to a depth of 3–5mm (⅛–¼in), depending on what you are using it for and use according to the relevant recipe instructions.

---

* For a vegetarian option, omit the lard and use just 175g (6¼oz/¾ cup) butter instead.

This recipe can be made successfully without the egg; although you might notice some flavour and textural difference. Use melted butter to brush the pastry prior to baking if you are avoiding egg completely.

PUFF PASTRY

Puff pastry doesn't need to be complicated. My aim is to simplify and demystify the process, making the many wondrous layers as easy to achieve as possible. Please do remember that professional kitchens accomplish great lamination using a pastry brake, but at home all we have is a rolling pin, patience and elbow grease! The only equipment I recommend having to hand (in addition to a rolling pin) is a sturdy ruler, a pizza wheel and a marker pen. A cool working environment is also highly beneficial.

Please don't be fooled into thinking you need a full day at home to make this pastry – the process of making the initial encasing dough through to the last fold can be done over many hours, or even a couple of days. However, there are a few points to bear in mind if this is the case.

MAKES 1 QUANTITY
Suitable for use in both sweet and savoury bakes

For the dough layer
250g (8¾ oz/1¾ cups plus 2 tablespoons) plain (all-purpose) flour, plus extra for dusting
1 teaspoon fine salt
25g (¾oz/1½ tablespoons) unsalted butter, melted but cooled
2½ teaspoons white wine vinegar
100g (3½oz) strained iced water

For the butter layer
200g (7oz/¾ cup plus 2 tablespoons) unsalted butter, fridge cold

For egg wash – if and when the recipe calls for it
1 egg yolk
boiling water

Place the flour, salt and melted butter into the bowl of a freestanding mixer. Using your hands, gently rub the butter into the flour **(1)**, until the texture resembles fine breadcrumbs.

Attach the dough hook to a mixer. Add the vinegar to the strained and weighed iced water. In a steady stream, pour this into the flour with the mixer running on a slow speed – mixing for 1 minute only. Turn out onto a lightly floured work surface, then bring together using your hands, discarding any crumbly dry pieces that aren't mixing into the dough easily. Wrap in cling film and place in the fridge for at least 1 hour.

On a lightly floured surface, roll the dough into a rectangle measuring approximately 30 x 20cm (12 x 8in). Shunt the four edges into straight lines (this is where the sturdy ruler comes in handy) **(2)**, then re-roll to an even thickness. Position the dough so that a shorter edge is nearest you.

Cut the block of butter across the width into nine equal slices. Lay the slices, edges touching, so that the bottom half

of the dough is covered, only leaving a very slight border of dough exposed. Using a knife, scrape the surface of the butter **(3)** so that all of the gaps between the slices become one, using the scraped butter to act like a filler.

When done, fold the uncovered half down, encasing the butter completely. Seal the three edges together by nipping the pastry together firmly **(4)**. If you have misjudged the fold a little and you have some excess pastry overhanging, simply trim it with a pizza wheel and discard that bit. Use the ruler to straighten all the edges **(5)** and shunt everything back into a neat rectangle.

Gently dust the pastry and the worktop with flour and re-position the pastry to prevent sticking. Gently press a rolling pin into the pastry across both the width and the length **(6)**, this will make the butter malleable.

Continued overleaf

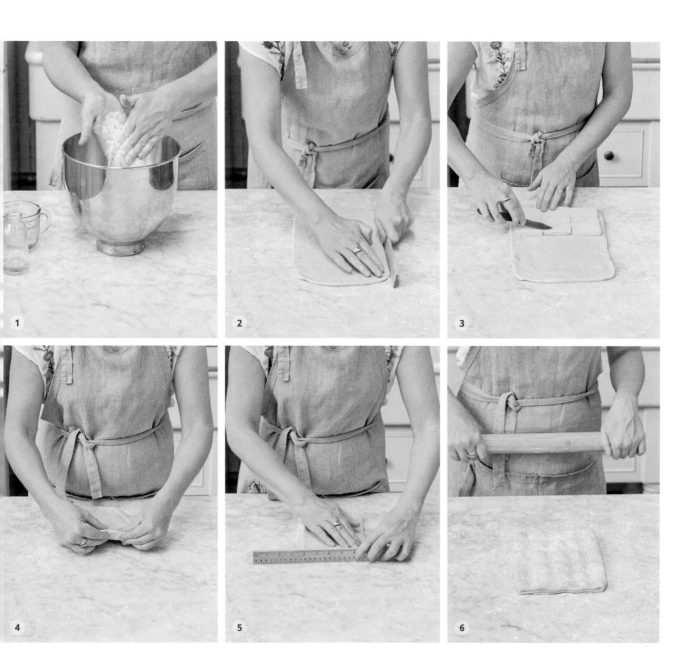

The pastry is now ready to be rolled out for use according to the relevant recipe instructions **(7)**, always with a shorter edge closest to you. There is no harm in turning the pastry over and switching top to bottom, but a short side must remain closest to you.

When rolled to the required size, shunt the edges to neaten **(8)** then fold the top half down to the two-thirds point. Bring the bottom third up and over it to create a single fold **(9)**. Again, use the trusted ruler to bring everything in line, then wrap the folded pastry in cling film. Using the marker pen, write 'x1' onto the cling film, referring to a single fold, and the time. Rest in the fridge for, at the very least, 1 hour.

Remove from the fridge (keeping the cling film) and place on a lightly floured surface. If the pastry has been in the fridge for longer than 1 hour, allow to stand at room temperature for 10–15 minutes, but if the kitchen is very hot, reduce the time accordingly. Gently press the pastry as previously instructed and pictured in image 6, then position it so one of the shorter sides is closest to you. Roll out as before, in an upwards and downwards motion only, to approximately 30 x 20cm (12 x 8in). Use a double fold this time. To do this, fold the top half down to the ¾ point

(10), then fold the remaining quarter up to meet it, lining up but not overlapping the pastry's edges neatly **(11)**. If the double fold was taken to the centre, a weak spot would be created, which could cause the layers to rupture during rolling. Now fold the pastry in half **(12)** by bringing the top half down to meet the bottom, keeping all edges neat and in line. Re-wrap in the same cling film as before and add 'x2', referring to the double fold, and the time, below the previous marking. Leave to rest in the fridge for at least 1 hour.

Repeat one more single and one more double fold, in that order, resting for a minimum of 1 hour between each fold and then a final hour after the last.

The pastry is now ready to be rolled out for use according to the relevant recipe instructions. Do remember, if the folded pastry has been in the fridge for longer than an hour, leave it to stand at room temperature for up to 15 minutes (see page 19), and use the pressing technique as in image 6 (see previous page) before gently rolling. It is also important to roll gently and rest occasionally, both to maintain the layers and prevent springback. The individual recipe will give specific instructions for baking, but whether it is baked under a weight or left to puff at will, you will love this

puff pastry. If it is made with the love and care that it deserves, it will not disappoint, I promise you.

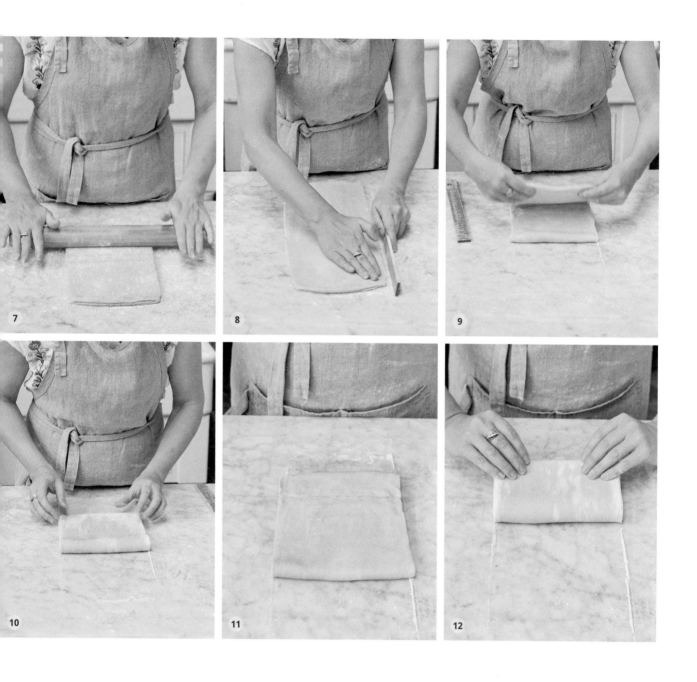

If unrolled puff or inverted puff pastry has been in the fridge for longer than an hour, allow to stand at room temperature for up to 15 minutes before rolling out. Reduce this time accordingly if the kitchen is hot.

INVERTED PUFF PASTRY

Inverted puff pastry isn't something you'd expect to see in a baking book aimed at the home cook. In fact, on researching it I often read that the challenge of making this pastry far outweighs its benefits. I disagree completely, and believe that if standard puff pastry can be made successfully at home, the inverted version can be, too. Is it worth the effort? Absolutely! The crunch you get from the finished pastry is just wonderful, and when used to make the Arlettes on page 192, let's just say the argument is over – you will be hooked from there on in.

Of course, there are some complications. With the butter being the outer encasing layer, hot hands will never make for a straightforward and easy task, but fret not, my tips and techniques will help even the most hot-handed bakers achieve those wonderfully crisp layers.

MAKES 1 QUANTITY
Suitable for both sweet and savoury bakes

For the encasing butter layer
180g (6⅓oz/¾ cup plus 2 teaspoons) unsalted butter, very cold and cut into 1cm (½in) cubes
80g (2¾oz/½ cup plus 1 tablespoon) strong white bread flour

For the dough layer
150g (5¼oz/1 cup) strong white bread flour, plus extra for dusting
½ teaspoon fine salt
45g (1½oz/3 tablespoons) unsalted butter, melted and cooled
juice of ¼ lemon
80g (2¾oz) strained iced water

To make the butter layer, place the cold cubed butter and the flour into the bowl of a freestanding mixer fitted with the paddle attachment. Mix on a medium speed for 1 minute, or until the two ingredients have combined. What you want is a stiff, buttery paste **(1)**, so do be careful not to overwork it. Lay out a large sheet of non-stick baking paper and place the paste on it. Cover with a second sheet and use a rolling pin and a sturdy ruler to flatten and manipulate the butter into a rectangle **(2)** measuring around 30 x 20cm (12 x 8in). Keep the butter in between the sheets of baking paper and place in the fridge for a minimum of 10 minutes, while preparing the next stage.

Place all of the dough layer ingredients into a large bowl – and bring together using a fork **(3)**. When well combined, roll out on a lightly floured work surface into a rectangle half the length and just short of the width of the butter layer – approximately 15 x 18cm (6 x 7in) **(4)**. Remove the butter layer from the fridge and position it so that a shorter side is closest to you. Lay the dough rectangle over the bottom half **(5)**, then fold the exposed butter downwards, using the paper underneath to help you **(6)**. Peel back the paper, leaving the butter in place, and seal the three edges by nipping the top and bottom layers together **(7 – overleaf)**. If your hands are hot, I would recommend plunging them into a bowl of iced water for a few minutes before touching the butter. Wrap the pastry loosely in the paper and then in cling film and place in the fridge for 30 minutes.

Continued overleaf

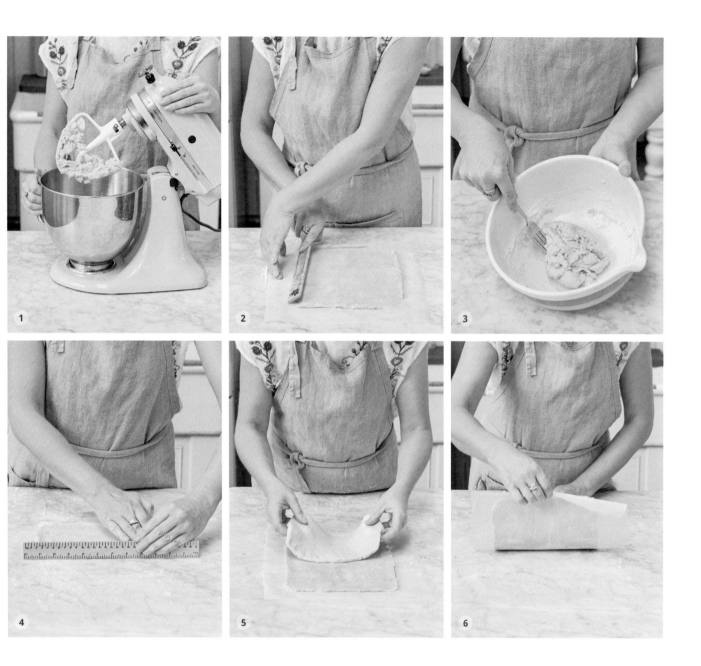

Lay out a sheet of non-stick baking paper and give it a very light dusting of flour. Unwrap the pastry (keep the wrapping) and place it on the paper, dusting with more flour. Gently press a rolling pin into the pastry, across both width and length **(8)**, this will help make the butter malleable.

The pastry is now ready to roll and fold. To do this successfully always roll on lightly floured non-stick baking paper and roll only using an upwards and downwards motion with a shorter edge always nearest you. There is no harm in turning the pastry over and switching top to bottom when doing this, as long as a short edge faces you throughout.

Roll out to the original rectangle of approximately 30 x 20cm (12 x 8in). If during rolling you feel that the butter is softening too much, simply return it to the fridge for 5 minutes on the paper, then try again. Use a sturdy ruler to shunt the edges into neat lines **(9)**. The pastry is now ready for the first fold.

To do this, bring the top half down to the two-thirds point **(10),** then bring the bottom third up and over it **(11)**, trying to keep the edges neat and in line with each other. Again, use the ruler to shunt it into position **(12)**. Re-wrap in the saved baking paper and cling film and use a marker pen to write 'x1', referring to the single fold, and the time. Rest in the fridge for, at the very least, 1 hour.

Remove from the fridge (keeping the wrappings) and place on a piece of lightly floured non-stick baking paper. If the pastry has been in the fridge for longer than 1 hour, allow to stand at room temperature for 10–15 minutes, or if the kitchen is very hot, reduce the time accordingly. Gently press the pastry as previously instructed in image 8, then position it so that one of the shortest sides is closest to you. Roll out as before, in an upwards and downwards motion, back to approximately 30 x 20cm (12 x 8in). Use a double fold this time (see page 18, steps 10, 11 and 12), keeping all the edges neat and in line. Re-wrap and add 'x2', referring to the double fold, and the time, below your previous marking. Leave to rest in the fridge for at least 1 hour.

Repeat one more single and one more double fold in that order, resting for a minimum of 1 hour between each, and then a final hour after the last fold. The pastry is now ready to be rolled out and baked according to the relevant recipe instructions. Do remember, if the folded pastry has been in the fridge for longer than an hour, leave it to stand at room temperature for up to 15 minutes (see page 19), and use the pressing technique as in image 8 before rolling. It is also important to roll gently and rest occasionally, both to maintain the layers and prevent springback.

Whether used to make Arlettes (see page 192) or even rolled through a pasta machine to create the perfect mille-feuille (see page 70), I do believe this pastry is special, and it never ceases to amaze people that you can make puff pastry with the butter on the outside!

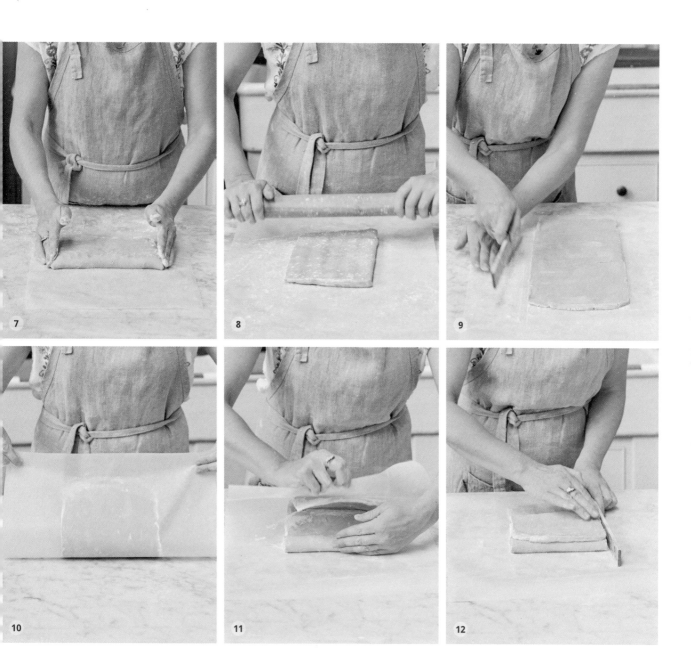

CHOUX PASTRY

I often hear people declare that choux pastry is the easiest pastry of all, yet I have found it to be the most frustrating to get right, and for a long time it was my Achilles heel. Personally, I find this pastry hard to control; once the oven door is closed, the fate of the piped paste is at the mercy of the steam generated during baking to give it lift. You can't open the door until the time is up, you just have to wait. Believe me when I say that I have had all kinds of comical shapes emerge from my oven, as well as under-baked, cracked and deflated pastry! However, after spending much time thinking over the process, and with lots of practice, I have finally learned to tame choux.

Ultimately the paste can't be too wet prior to baking – and let's just say a craquelin top (a simple dough made from butter, sugar and flour) can hide a multitude of piping sins!

MAKES 1 QUANTITY

125ml (4fl oz/½ cup) warm water
125ml (4fl oz/½ cup) full-fat milk, at room temperature
100g (3½oz/1 cup minus 1 tablespoon) unsalted butter, cut into 1cm (½in) cubes, at room temperature
150g (5¼oz/1 cup) strong white bread flour
½ teaspoon fine salt
1 teaspoon caster (superfine) sugar
4 eggs

For egg wash – if and when the recipe calls for it
1 egg yolk
boiling water

Place the water, milk and butter in a medium saucepan and gently heat until the butter melts. When fully melted, increase the heat and tip in the flour, salt and sugar **(1)** and stir together until the mixture becomes a thick paste **(2)**. Keep stirring until the choux leaves the sides and base of the pan – the paste should follow the spoon around the pan as you stir. Turn the heat to low, then stir continuously for 5 minutes. Don't cut short on this time – it is important – as this stage helps some of the moisture to evaporate, leaving behind a thicker, drier paste **(3)**, which is essential.

Transfer to the bowl of a freestanding mixer fitted with a paddle attachment **(4)** and beat on a slow speed until the paste has cooled, with no sign of any steam rising from the bowl. With the mixer still running, add one of the eggs **(5)**, then when – and only when – the first egg has been fully incorporated into the paste, add the next. Repeat until all of the eggs have been added and a thick yet glossy paste with a stiff dropping consistency remains **(6)**.

Pipe, top and bake according to the relevant recipe instructions.

VIENNOISERIE PASTRY

My purpose here was to write a recipe so that you could enjoy freshly baked Viennoiserie with your morning coffee, without the need to set the alarm and start baking at daft o'clock. It can be done, but only by making the pastry in the afternoon the day before baking, and slowing the rise by placing them in the fridge overnight. I have included a timeline to follow, which can be shifted to suit the time of day at which the baked pastry is required.

The best friend you'll have when making this pastry is a cool environment. Never before has a cold kitchen, a cold rolling pin and a cool work surface been more favourable.

MAKES 1 QUANTITY
Suitable for both sweet and savoury bakes

For the dough layer
250g (8¾oz/1¾ cups) strong white bread flour, plus extra for sprinkling and dusting
35g (1¼oz/3 tablespoons) caster (superfine) sugar
¼ teaspoon fine salt
1 teaspoon dried easy bake yeast
65g (2¼oz) cold full-fat milk
65g (2¼oz) cold water
25g (¾oz/1½ tablespoons) unsalted butter, very soft

For the butter layer
140g (5oz/²⁄₃ cup minus 2 teaspoons) unsalted butter, fridge-cold

For egg wash – if and when the recipe calls for it
1 egg yolk
boiling water

Place the flour, sugar, salt and yeast into the bowl of a freestanding mixer. Attach the dough hook and combine briefly. Mix together the milk and water, and with the mixer running on a slow speed, pour into the bowl in a steady continuous stream. Mix for 4 minutes only, after which the dough should be cohesive and the sides of the bowl clean. Start to add small pieces of the soft butter, one piece at a time **(1)**, still mixing on a slow speed. Only when each piece of butter has been incorporated should another be added. Continue as before until all of the butter has been used – this should take around 5 minutes. Sprinkle over a dessertspoon of flour and give it a 30-second mix until combined. Switch off the mixer, turn the dough out onto a lightly floured work surface and roll flat to approximately 1cm (½in) depth. Wrap in cling film and place in the fridge for 1½ hours.

Prepare the butter layer by slicing the block across the width into eight equal-sized slices. Lay these 4 x 2 onto a piece of non-stick baking paper **(2)** and place in the fridge.

On a lightly floured surface, roll the dough into a rectangle measuring approximately 30 x 20cm (12 x 8in) **(3)**. Shunt the four edges into straight lines using a ruler **(4)**, then re-roll to an even thickness. Position so that a shorter edge is nearest you. Remove the butter from the fridge, then invert onto the bottom half of the rolled dough, peeling back the paper **(5)**. Using a knife, scrape the surface of the butter and use the scrapings to smooth over the gaps between the butter slices **(6)**, making them into one large slice.

Now fold down the upper half of the dough, covering the butter completely. If you have misjudged the fold a little and excess pastry is overhanging, simply trim with a pizza wheel.

Continued overleaf

Seal the three edges, nipping them together firmly **(7)**, then shunt back into shape using the ruler **(8)**. Wrap in cling film and return to the fridge for 30 minutes.

Lightly dust the worktop with flour and lay the pastry on it. Gently press a rolling pin into the pastry across both width and length **(9)**, helping to make the butter malleable. The pastry is now ready to roll back to the original size of 30 x 20cm (12 x 8in).

To create the layers successfully, it is important to roll using an upwards and downwards motion only, always with a shorter edge closest to you. There is no harm in turning the pastry over and switching top to bottom, but a short side must remain closest to you. When rolled to the required size, shunt the edges to neaten **(10)**, then fold the top half down to the two-thirds point **(11)**. Bring the bottom third up and over it **(12)**, creating a single fold. Wrap the folded pastry in cling film and, using a marker pen, write 'x1' onto it, referring to the single fold, and the time. These markings are a valuable reminder of what stage you are at and what time the next fold is due. Rest in the fridge and set a timer for 1 hour.

Remove from the fridge (keeping the cling film) and place on a lightly floured surface. Repeat the rolling and folding process from steps 9 through to 12, twice more, resting in the fridge for an hour between each and for a final hour before rolling and cutting, setting your timer as a vital reminder.

When rolling to cut and shape, it is important that the kitchen is cool. It is surprising how quickly the dough can rise, if that happens the buttery layers will become exposed and can be pushed out when rolling. To roll, do so in short bursts – roll, leave for 1 minute, then roll again (and so on) until the pastry is fully rolled. Allowing the pastry to relax between rolling prevents the dough from springing back. Over-forceful rolling can also rupture the layers and will undo all of the work that has been put in up to that point. I find it easier to roll on marble or granite for this stage, due to the minimal amount of flour needed. The cold, slick surface helps to hold the dough in place, preventing springback. When fully rolled out to a 5mm (¼in) thickness, pop in the freezer for 10 minutes, then cut and shape according to the recipe instructions.

When proving, leave at room temperature covered with cling film for up to 2 hours (or up to 3 hours if they have been in the fridge overnight – see timeline below), until doubled in size. It is important that the room is only warm, not hot, and make sure the pastries are away from sunlight or a heat source. Both would melt the butter.

Follow the relevant recipe for baking instructions.

TIMELINE FOR SAME-DAY PASTRIES

07.00	make the dough
07.15	make the butter layer, then place both in the fridge for 1½ hours
08.45	roll and create the first fold; at 09.00, place in the fridge for 1 hour
10.00	roll and create the second fold; at 10.15, place in the fridge for 1 hour
11.15	roll and create the third fold; at 11.30, place in the fridge for 1 hour
12.30	roll, cut and shape the pastries
13.00	allow to prove at room temperature for up to 2 hours
	Between 14.30 and 15.00 – Bake

TIMELINE FOR MORNING PASTRIES

17.00	make the dough
17.15	make the butter layer, then place both in the fridge for 1½ hours
18.45	roll and create the first fold; at 19.00, place in the fridge for 1 hour
20.00	roll and create the second fold; at 20.15, place in the fridge for 1 hour
21.15	roll and create the third fold; at 21.30, place in the fridge for 1 hour
22.30	roll, cut and shape the pastries
23.00	place in the fridge for 8 hours (overnight)
07.00	remove from the fridge and allow to prove at room temperature for up to *3 hours
	Between 09.30 and 10.00 – Bake

* The extra hour needed for proving after the fridge resting is simply giving the dough time to reach room temperature first, however, if you feel the pastries have doubled in size prior to the 3 hours, go ahead and bake them sooner.

Refer to the relevant recipe for any shaping, baking and filling instructions.

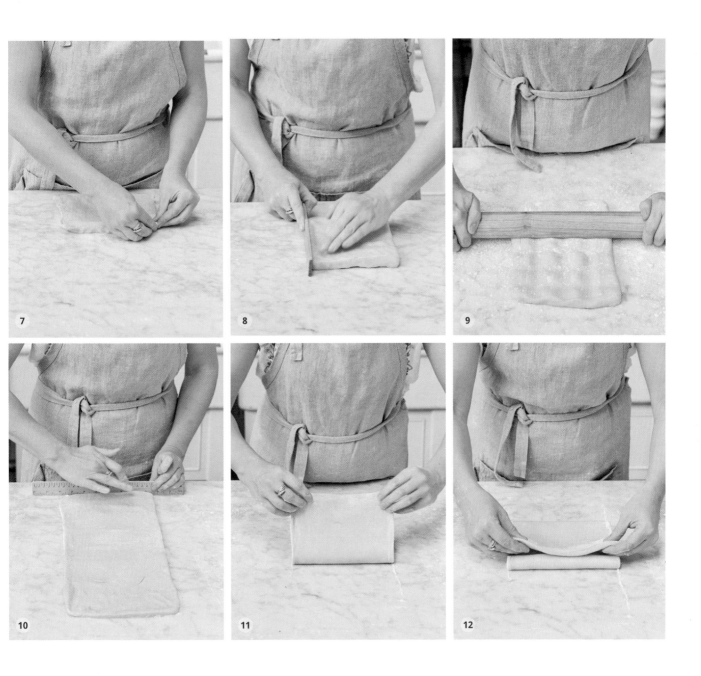

These two full pages of text may have put many off already, but like any good thing, this pastry really is worth the faff.

SHEET PASTRY

Please don't just flick past this page, making sheet pastry is simpler than you may think, and it is easier to achieve than filo, in the respect that it is stretched rather than rolled to paper-thin transparency. I'm not saying this pastry is a doddle, but it is something you'll get better at with practice, and believe me, I say this from experience. The trick is to stretch the dough little by little, resting between each stretch until eventually an incredible sheet of see-through pastry lies before you. It is very satisfying once you have the knack, and totally worth the effort.

You will need a lint-free cloth laid smoothly over a small table or similar, measuring approximately 100 x 50cm (3ft x 20in). I use my coffee table, which has proven to be the perfect size for one quantity of dough.

MAKES 1 QUANTITY
Suitable for both sweet and savoury bakes

250g (8¾oz/1¾ cups plus 2 tablespoons) plain (all-purpose) flour, plus extra for dusting
1 teaspoon fine salt
1 egg
100g (3½oz) warm water, around 50°C (122°F)
1 tablespoon grapeseed oil, plus extra for rubbing

Place the flour, salt, egg, water and oil into a bowl and mix together using a fork **(1)**. When the dough is mostly cohesive, turn out onto a lightly floured work surface and knead for 3 minutes **(2)**, stretching and pulling, rolling beneath hands. When smooth, shape into a ball and rub all over with a little more oil **(3)**, then wrap in cling film and rest in the fridge for 30 minutes. It is important to start the next process precisely after the 30-minute resting. I have found this to be the optimum time for the dough to be stretched. I don't know why, no doubt there will be a scientific reason behind it! I recommend setting a timer after placing it in the fridge, so you don't forget.

Lightly yet evenly dust the tablecloth with flour and rub in well. Place the ball of dough in the centre of the table, dust with flour and start to roll out, trying to keep the shape rectangular **(4)**. As the dough stretches it is important to rest occasionally for 30-second intervals, to allow the dough to relax – which makes rolling easier. Continue to roll until the surface area has at least doubled, after which time all further stretching must be done by hand.

Snag-free hands are essential here, so if needed do remove any of your rings and clip sharp nails to prevent tearing. Start the stretching by lifting an edge of the dough and gently and slowly pull the dough outwards **(5)**, until it stretches. Move around to another area and do the same, continuing around the table until the pastry has stretched out towards its edges **(6)**. Do be patient, only returning to a previously stretched area after 30 seconds or more. Small holes or tears may appear, but worry not – a perfect stretch only comes with practice and usually these snags won't be noticed when the pastry is used later.

Continue to stretch until the dough hangs over the table's edges, to secure it in place. Allow the pastry to dry for 5 minutes before trimming all around the outer edge using a pizza wheel. Discard the excess.

Some recipes will call for the pastry to be rubbed with cornflour (cornstarch) **(7)** or cut into sheets **(8)**. Some will call for a lengthy drying time and others may need to be generously brushed with butter. Whatever the use, stand back and look at what you have created **(9)** from a few basic ingredients and some patience.

Refer to individual recipes for further instructions on use.

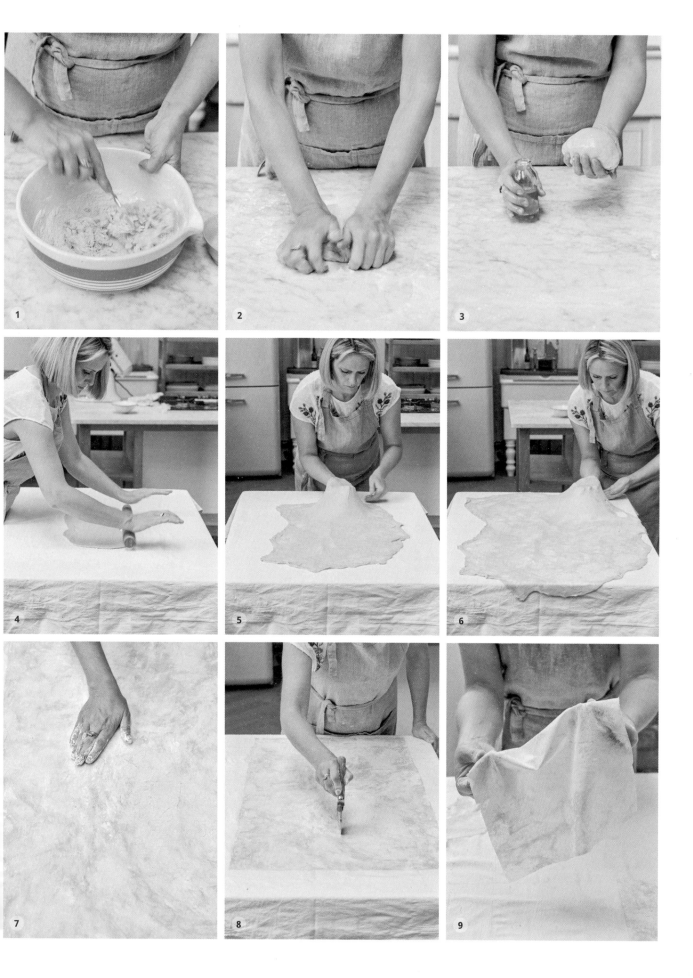

SALTED & SWEET GLUTEN-FREE PASTRY

I won't sugar-coat this, getting this pastry right was a challenge! After all, pastry relies on gluten for its stretch, which in turn enables us to shape pastries easily and give each variety its unique texture. Without gluten, pliability is lost and the texture when eating becomes unpleasant, even powder-like.

However, with so many people now suffering from gluten intolerance, and some just preferring not to eat gluten, I felt that a decent alternative pastry was a much-needed addition to this book. After endless amounts of researching and testing, I do believe this coeliac-friendly recipe is great, both in taste and texture – which, if you have tasted gluten-free pastry before, you will know that this is quite a revelation!

MAKES 1 QUANTITY

35g (1¼oz) ground almonds (for a stronger flavour, use ground hazelnuts)
40g (1½oz) brown rice flour, plus 1 tablespoon, if needed
50g (1¾oz) juwar (sorghum) flour
35g (1¼oz) tapioca flour
30g (1oz/scant ¼ cup) cornflour (cornstarch), plus extra for dusting
15g (½oz) amaranth seeds, ground (*see note)
½ teaspoon fine salt
115g (4oz/½ cup) unsalted butter, very cold, cut into 1cm (½in) cubes
1 egg yolk
50ml (1⅔fl oz/3½ tablespoons) cold milk

For egg wash (if stated in the recipe)
1 egg yolk
boiling water

In the bowl of a freestanding mixer, place all of the dry ingredients **(1)** and the butter, then attach the paddle. Mix on a medium speed until the butter has been incorporated into the flour **(2)** – bigger, unevenly distributed pieces of butter are fine, as this will help the pastry to flake and be less cardboard-like when baked (as is characteristic of gluten-free pastry). Add the egg yolk and the milk **(3)** and continue to mix until a cohesive dough forms **(4)** – this should take only 30–60 seconds, depending on your mixer. If the pastry seems overly wet at this point, add an extra tablespoon of brown rice flour and re-mix.

Lay out a long sheet of cling film and place the pastry on one half, then flatten it down with the palms of your hands and fold the remaining cling film over the top, fully encasing the dough. Roll out between the cling film **(5)** to an approximate depth of 5mm (¼in), trying your best to keep it in a circular shape. Place in the fridge for at least an hour to rest.

After resting, lay out a sheet of non-stick baking paper and dust it with cornflour (corn starch). Transfer the pastry to the paper and dust the surface with a little more cornflour. Top with a second sheet of baking paper and roll out between the papers **(6)**, lifting and replacing the papers from time to time to prevent sticking. An additional light dusting of cornflour will do little harm.

The pastry is now ready to use according to the relevant recipe instructions – whether to line tart tins or simply cut and baked to make the base of a tarte fine.

* To grind the amaranth seeds, place a larger amount than you need into a spice grinder, pestle and mortar, or similar, and blitz or pummel until the seeds become floury but aren't yet reduced to a powder – this texture will help the finished pastry have some crunch. Weigh out the 15g (½oz) needed and keep the rest in an airtight container for future use.
* For a sweet version, simply add 20g (¾oz) icing (powdered) sugar and omit the salt.

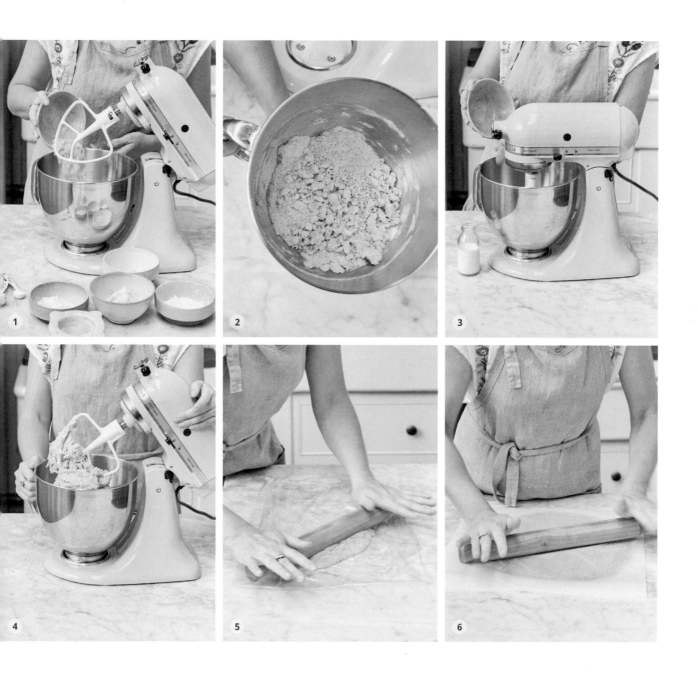

To line baking tins, the same method can be used as shown
on page 38, however you may find it easier to simply push the
dough into the tin using your fingertips.

SWEET & SALTED VEGAN PASTRY

I was dubious about being able to create a vegan pastry – after all, butter is high on my list of 'favourite ingredients of all time'. I've used coconut oil as the alternative to butter here, which works well with the coconut milk. This particular pastry is excellent when used for the Mango and Coconut Cream Tartlets on page 66, but if you want to make that a fully vegan recipe, substitute the cream cheese with a vegan coconut-based variety.

I urge non-vegan readers to try making this pastry too, as the crisp texture that the oil provides is quite special and should definitely not be overlooked just because it has no butter – and you are hearing that from butter's number one fan! It really is delicious.

MAKES 1 QUANTITY

230g (8oz/1¾ cups) plain (all-purpose) flour
80g (2¾oz) refrigerated, solidified coconut oil, coarsely grated
50g (1¾oz) Trex (vegan baking fat) or preferred brand, cut into 1cm (½in) cubes
50g (1¾oz/⅓ cup) icing (powdered) sugar
½ teaspoon fine salt
3 tablespoons unsweetened coconut milk

In the bowl of a freestanding mixer, place the flour, solidified grated coconut oil and Trex **(1)** and attach the paddle beater. Mix on a medium speed until both the oil and fat have been incorporated into the flour. Small lumps of the coconut oil may still be visible, which is fine **(2)**. Add the icing (powdered) sugar **(3)** (if using) and mix for a few seconds before adding your preferred plant-based milk. Continue to mix until a cohesive dough forms **(4)** – this should only take 30 seconds to a minute, depending on your mixer. Turn out the pastry on a work surface and bring together with your hands **(5)**.

Lay out a long sheet of cling film and place the pastry on one half of the length. Flatten the pastry with the palms of your hands, then fold the remaining cling film over the top, fully encasing the dough. Roll out between the cling film **(6)** to an approximate depth of 5mm (¼in), trying to keep it in a circular shape. Place in the fridge for at least an hour before using.

After resting, roll out between two sheets of non-stick baking paper and use according to the relevant recipe instructions.

For tips on successfully lining tins, blind baking and trimming a pastry case, see page 38.

---

*For a salted version, omit the icing (powdered) sugar and add ½ teaspoon fine salt.
*Rice or other nut milks could be used.

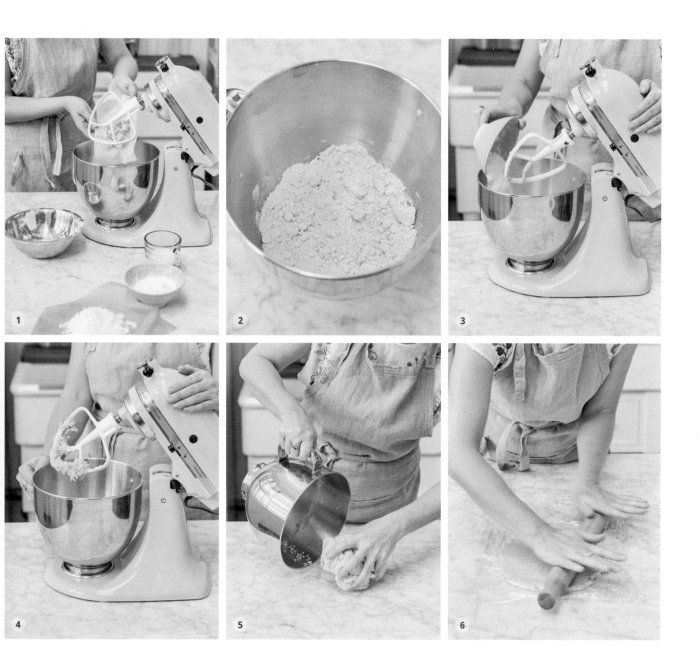

ROLLING PASTRY THROUGH A PASTA MACHINE

A pasta machine* may seem like an odd piece of equipment to have ready for use when making pies and pastries, but it can be a very useful one. Not only will it aid in rolling the pastry to a consistent depth without overworking, it can also be extremely handy for cutting into neat strips to be used for latticing, and intricate décor – see pages 40, 63, 99 and 142 for some ideas, and page 42 for further instruction. I sometimes even roll laminated pastry through the machine (see page 70) to achieve a consistent rise, but this does have to be done with caution.

There are a few factors that need to be considered prior to rolling any sort of pastry through a pasta roller; the most important is that the pastry is at a good working temperature. Too warm and it will get stuck between the rollers, too cold and it will crack before it has passed all the way through. It is simply a case of trial and error and something that comes with practice. Start off with a small piece to test how it will roll through, before rolling larger quantities.

Flour the roller before passing any variety of pastry through the machine, and do remember never to wash the pasta machine afterwards. Pass the pastry through the machine only once (unless rolling thinner), to prevent overworking. Any remaining pastry will dry and crumble out on its own. Washing will cause the rollers and the wheels inside the machine to rust, and that will be the end of that!

Roll with the machine set to its widest setting, this is actually perfectly thin enough for pastry. If, however, dainty petit fours cases are needed (see page 66) I would take advantage of the tighter settings to roll very thin pastry, thus creating a very delicate, melt-in-the-mouth pastry case when baked. Be quite swift when rolling – get the job done. Once the pastry enters the rollers, keep turning the handle without hesitation until it has passed through. If the rolling is intermittent the pastry can develop grooves, creating weak spots, which may cause problems later on.

I have rolled both sweet and salted shortcrust, hot water, vegan, puff and inverted puff pastry through my pasta roller to great success, and therefore consider my pasta machine an essential piece of baking equipment.

*The pasta attachment on a KitchenAid or another free-standing mixer can also be used.

BLIND BAKING

I am often asked to share my tips on how to blind bake pastry cases successfully. The best advice that I can give would simply be: take care and time over all of the stages involved – from making the dough through to the final bake. If every stage is done with patience, the pastry case will be crisp and golden and there will be minimal or zero shrinkage.

Surprisingly, there are quite a few stages involved, and I urge you to not rush through or skip any of them, otherwise both pastry and pastry case will undoubtedly suffer. This method works well when using both the sweet and savoury shortcrust, vegan and gluten-free pastries from this book.

After the dough has been made (see the individual recipes for specifics), it must be rested in the fridge for a minimum of one hour with the exception of Salted Shortcrust. I have seen so many bakers place the dough into the fridge shaped into a thick slab or ball, which I advise against. When the chilled pastry hardens, it becomes difficult to roll flat and the extra effort needed will result in overworking. This can cause the pastry to shrink during baking and, not only that, the texture will suffer, too. To avoid this, encase the dough between cling film and flatten it with a few strokes of a rolling pin **(1)**. It will then be much easier to roll out properly after being chilled and rested.

When ready to roll out fully, do so between two sheets of non-stick baking paper **(2)**. Rolling this way requires paper, no extra dustings of flour, which can change the dough significantly. It is also a nifty way to transfer the rolled pastry to the tin, with minimal handling – which is great, particularly for the hot-handed. Simply invert the pastry to cover the tin then peel back the baking paper **(3)**.

To create a neat pastry case, it is important to line the tin properly, easing the pastry into every corner, fold and fluted edge of the tin **(4)**. When in place, wrap a small piece of pastry in cling film and use this to gently mould the pastry into place **(5)**. To prevent shrinkage, leave an overhanging edge around the top of the tin, 2cm (¾in) being enough. Trim off the excess (I use scissors), saving any scraps for another use. It is important to chill and rest the pastry again prior to baking, resting for a minimum of 30 minutes in the fridge.

To blind bake, preheat the oven to 180°C (350°F), Gas Mark 4 and place a baking sheet in the oven, unless otherwise stated within the recipe. Scrunch up a piece of non-stick baking paper, a little larger than the tin being used then unfold it and place on top of the pastry **(6)**. Fill the case with baking beans, dried rice or lentils, or a mixture of all 3 **(7)**. It is important to fill all the way to the top of the tin, as this will prevent the pastry from coming away from the sides during baking and the extra weight will stop the base from lifting. Bake in the oven for 20 minutes, then spoon out the beans and remove the paper.

The base of the pastry case may still look a little raw towards the centre, which is fine. Gently prick the base with a fork and return to the oven for a further 5 minutes until all of the rawness has baked, yet the colour is still relatively pale. It is important to check the case for any holes or slight cracks. If any are visible, use the leftover pastry to fill these in carefully.

Make an egg wash by mixing an egg yolk with a few drops of boiling water and use this to glaze the pastry case, making sure to brush both pastry base and sides. Not all of the egg wash will be needed.

Return to the oven for another 15–20 minutes, or until the pastry case is deep golden, crisp and cooked through. Don't be alarmed if the overhanging edge seems burnt, this will be shaved off and discarded. Allow to cool completely in the tin.

The best tool for trimming away the overhanging edge is a vegetable peeler, one with a swivelling blade. Use the peeler to gently shave the pastry, until the top of the tin has been reached **(8)**. Brush away any crumbs that have fallen inside the pastry case **(9)**. The case is now ready to be filled and served, or filled and re-baked depending on the recipe instructions.

The baked case can be kept in an airtight container for up to 3 days if it is not needed straight away.

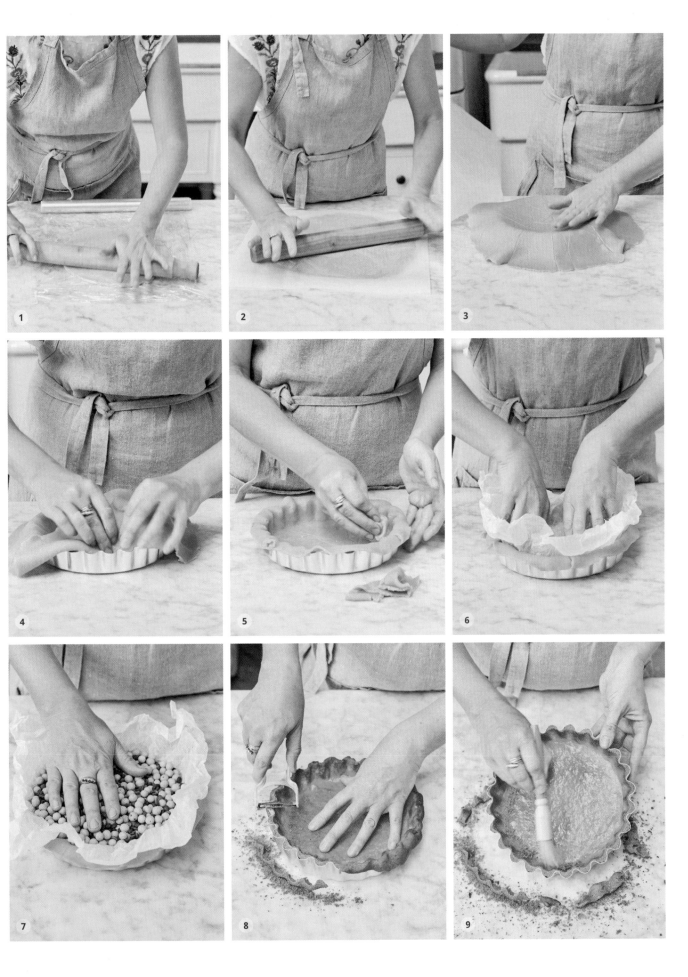

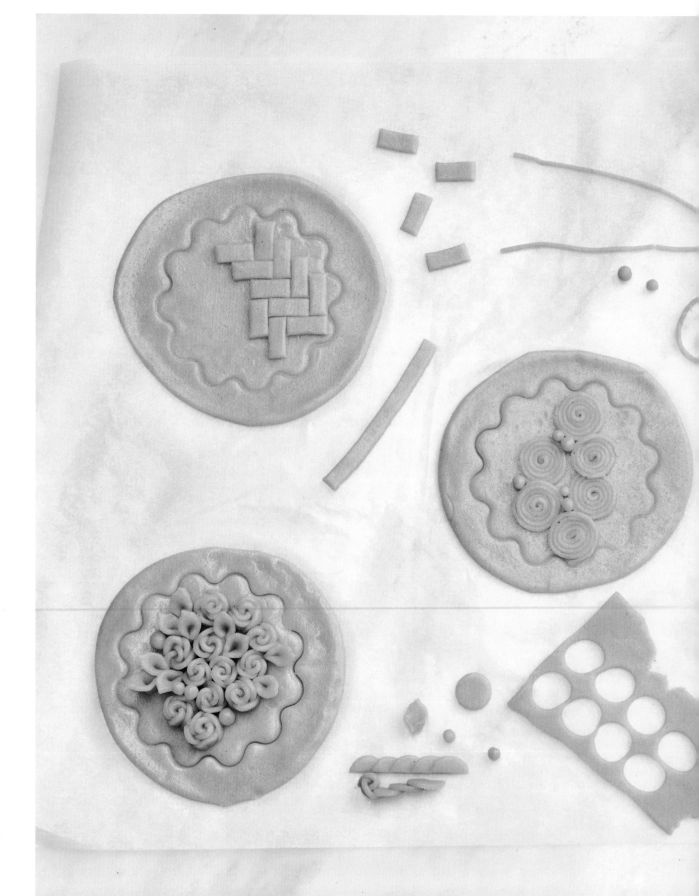

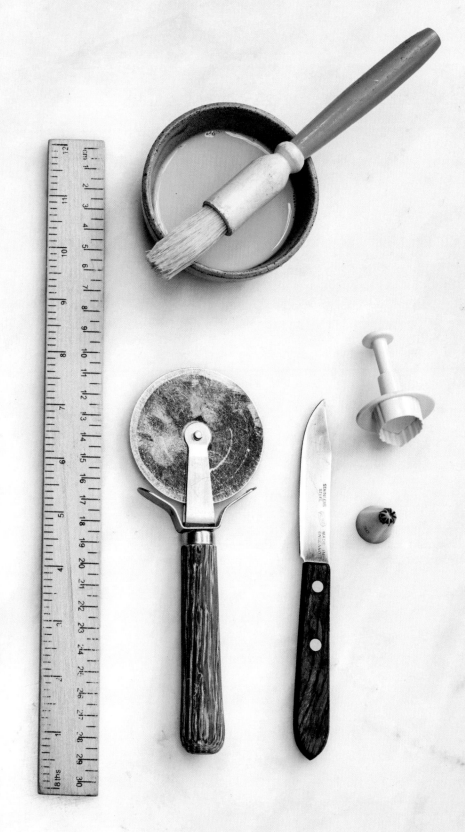

DECORATIVE TECHNIQUES

Decorating pie tops is a favourite pastime of mine. I find that creative freedom gives an open and clear mind, the quiet time spent faffing about, soothing. Although an aesthetically pleasing pie top is charming, what is most important is that it bakes well. There is little point spending an hour or more making a pretty pie crust if it doesn't taste as good as it looks. Here are some tips on how to re-create some of the finishes that I have used within the book.

For a fully covered pie and one that has intricate décor, I always lay the flowers, tiles, spirals or lattices on top of a thinly rolled piece of pastry, then transfer the finished design to the pre-filled pie base afterwards. The rolled pastry needs to be thin, as the décor laid on top will be like an additional layer, so do bear that in mind. A pastry brush and some egg wash will be needed for all.

To start, roll out some pastry, nice and thin, to a size larger than the tart/pie tin being used and lay it upon a piece of non-stick baking paper (this will aid in transferring the pastry lid to the base later). Use the selected tin to indent the pastry in order to mark out where the perimeter of the lid will be. This will be the guide on where to build the design up to.

- *For the parquet effect:* A little maths may be required to make the tiles fit neatly together, unless a specialist cutter is used. I prefer to hand-cut my pastry tiles, as it gives me more freedom to create the design that I want. Either way, the method remains the same. Roll, measure and cut sufficient pastry tiles to lay across the marked-out pastry lid. Lightly brush a small area of the pastry and start to lay the tiles, side by side, in the pattern of choice. Continue to lay the tiles until the edges of the marked circle have been reached.

- *For the rose garden effect:* A round cutter is needed, the circumference depending on the size of the rose required. For the small roses as pictured on page 40, I have used the wide end of a piping nozzle. Roll out the pastry and cut some circles from it. Lay at least five circles, slightly overlapping each other, into a row, working left to right. Cut the row in half, then roll up each in half from the left side, creating the rose. Trim the base of the flower so that it will sit closer to the pastry lid. Repeat to create as many roses as desired. Leaves can be cut using specialist cutters, or hand-shaped. Remember to secure each flower or leaf in place with some egg wash.

- *For the spiral effect*: Super thin strips of pastry are required here, and although these can be hand-cut, I find the best way to achieve this is to pass the rolled pastry through a pasta machine, and then through the spaghetti cutter (see page 36). Brush the area of the pie lid that the spiral will be laid onto with egg wash. Curl the very end of a cut strip of pastry, then lay it onto the egg wash. Gently swirl around the central curl until a spiral forms. To make the spiral larger, simply build out the layers using more strips.

When you are happy with the design, the pie top must be chilled sufficiently before transferring it to the base of the pie. Allow it to chill in the fridge for a minimum of 30 minutes, or if you are short on time, pop it in the freezer for 5 minutes. When the pastry has stiffened, hold it over the prepared pie base and peel away the baking paper, placing the pie lid in position. To neaten, press down firmly around the edge of the tart tin, thus cutting away the excess, unused pastry and securing the lid to the base in the process.

It is important that the pastry is cold before baking, so that the décor will stay the same during baking. Therefore, if transferring the lid to the base has taken some time, place the pie back into the fridge until chilled.

Preheat the oven, as per the recipe instructions, then egg wash the surface of the pie lid, taking time and care when doing so, I find a small artist brush useful here. Add a couple of steam holes, if needed, then sprinkle with caster (superfine) sugar, if desired, and bake in the pre-heated oven as per the recipe timings.

Be vigilant during baking, if the décor is raised in parts, these will colour and bake much more quickly than the rest. A careful placement of kitchen foil on any parts that are colouring too quickly will aid with an even bake.

ALTERNATIVE & CREATIVE PASTRY AND FILLINGS

The key overleaf was designed to further encourage creative baking – a way by which to turn a book comprized of 56 set recipes, using 10 different pastries, into a book with a much wider scope. Given the possibility that both pastries and fillings within a set recipe are interchangeable, the only real limit on variations is your imagination. There are, of course, a few factors that need to be considered if you do decide to use a different pastry or filling, but with careful thought before baking, pretty much any variation can be achieved. Simply use the tips and techniques given throughout these pages and apply them to your experimental baking.

My hope is that the key will provide inspiration, spark ingenuity and allow you to bake outside of the 'pastry' box. Some great examples are choux and viennoiserie – these pastries need not be reserved only for sweet fillings, they are, in fact, a revelation when rolled, stuffed or filled with something unusual and savoury. Likewise, the crunchy pastry topping used on the Oxtail Scrunch Pot Pie on page 158 is heavenly sat atop the sweet and fruity Boozy Cherry Liquor pie filling on page 62.

I do suggest getting to know each pastry well before starting to experiment, as each type is special and unique in texture, taste and structural durability. Understanding how each pastry tastes and behaves during baking will help you in your recipe development and will ensure that your experiments will be successful and delicious every time.

Please don't be tempted to skip using the gluten-free or vegan pastries should they not be a necessity in your own specific diet – both are excellent for all, their flavour and texture adding interest and unique qualities to every dish they are used in. It is a fact that one of my favourite recipes within this book is one that uses the gluten-free pastry, which is something I never imagined possible when I started writing this book.

If you do follow a gluten-free or vegan diet, please be aware that in the recipes where I have suggested this pastry as an alternative, adjustments to the filling(s) may be necessary. For vegetarians, the hot water pastry can be successfully made using all butter, instead of the suggested ratio of lard to butter.

Finally, if you want to switch a pastry from sweet to savoury, please see the individual pastry recipe for guidance.

With that, I will leave you to create. Enjoy the freedom that experimenting with food gives, and do remember to tag me @julie_jonesuk with #thepastryschool if you share your creations on Instagram!

HERE ARE A FEW IDEAS TO GET YOU STARTED:

1. Use the lychee and violet crème with the macerated fruit from the recipe on page 60 to fill mini sweet shortcrust pastry shells, like the ones shown on page 66. Top each with an edible flower and serve as petit fours. So pretty.

2. Blind bake puff pastry under weight, as in the recipe for Vanilla Slices on page 83, then instead of using the vanilla crème, use the chocolate and caramel fillings from the éclair recipe on page 97. Heavenly.

3. For the Onion and Egg Tartlets on page 134, use sheet pastry to make crunchy cups, as in the recipe on page 80, however, make larger cups using a Yorkshire pudding tray to accommodate the fillings. The textural contrast would be amazing.

4. Convert the Chocolate, Pecan and Brazil Nut Bars on page 124 to gluten-free. Use the sweet gluten-free pastry recipe on page 32 and swap the plain (all-purpose) flour in the filling for ½ teaspoon of cornflour (corn starch). Easy.

5. For a variation on the Oxtail Scrunch Pot Pie on page 158, use salted shortcrust pastry instead. Blind bake a pastry case, fill with the oxtail filling, top with a pastry lid and bake. Equally as delicious, just more conventional in texture and appearance.

KEY

- ● Alternative: the highlighted pastry can be used successfully as an alternative to the one shown in the recipe
- ○ Creative: the highlighted pastry could be used to encase, top or sandwich the filling in the recipe to create a unique and experimental bake
- ✶ Original: indicates the pastry used within the recipe shown

Alterations may be required to make suggested recipes completely vegan, vegetarian and gluten free.

If switching a pastry from a sweet to savoury please see individual pastry recipes.

	CH	GF	HW	IP	P	S	SH	SW	VE	VIE
Fruit										
Apple Rose Tart (2020)		●						✶		
Apple Tarte Tatin		●		●	✶		●	●		
Apricot and Vanilla Danish with Fennel Seed Caramel	○	○		●	●		○	○		✶
Boozy Cherry Liquor Pie	○	○			○		○	✶	●	○
Gluten-free Lemon Meringue Pie		✶								
Lychee and Violet Craquelin Choux	✶	○		○	○		○	○		○
Mango and Coconut Cream Tartlets	○	●			○		○	●	✶	○
Poached Peach, Zabaglione and Sweet Strudel Scrunch							✶			
Raspberry and Rose Gin Mille Feuille	○	●		✶	●		○	●		○
Roasted Rhubarb and Raspberry Tart	○	●			○		○	✶	●	○
Salted Caramel Banana Tarte Tatins		●		●	✶		●	●		
Cream & Cheese										
Butterscotch Crunch with Crystallized Rosemary		●					✶	●		○
Chamomile Panna Cotta Tart		●						✶		
Double Choc' Éclairs with Vanilla Caramel	✶	○		○	○		○	○		○
Fromage Blanc, Honeycomb and Fig Viennoiserie	○	○		●	●		○	○		✶
Goat's Cheese and Fennel Jam Galette		●	●			✶	○			○
Nana Maud's Custard Tart								✶		
Pastiera Napoletana								✶		
Super Slow Onion and Gruyère Tart			●			✶	○			
Tartiflette Pies		○	✶			●	○			○
Vanilla Slices	○	●		●	✶		○	●		○
Nuts										
Chocolate, Cherry and Almond Pithiviers		○		✶	●		○	○		○
Chocolate, Pecan and Brazil Nut Bars		●					○	✶		○
Frangipane, Persimmon and Grape Tart		●						✶		
Paris Brest with Cherries and Dipped Hazelnuts	✶	○		○	○		○	○		○
Peanut and Potato Satay Bites		○					✶		○	
Pine Nut Praline, Rum and Raisin Pinwheels	○	○		●	●		○	○		✶
Pistachio Tart with Rhubarb Tiles		●						✶		
Treacle Tart Deluxe		●						✶		
Walnut, Pear and Regalis Tarte Fines	○	✶	●	●	○	●	○			○

CH choux   **S** sheet

GF gluten free   **SH** salt

HW hot water   **SW** sweet

IP inverted puff   **VE** vegan

P puff   **VIE** viennoiserie

	CH	GF	HW	IP	P	S	SH	SW	VE	VIE
Vegetables										
Beetroot Tarte Tatin		●	●	●	✳	●	●		●	
Celeriac and Apple Tarte Fines	○	✳	●	●	○	●	○		●	○
Chestnut and Mushroom Rotolo	○	○	○			○	✳			○
Griddled Greens, Cauliflower and Lemon Triangles		○			○	○	✳		○	○
Leek, Potato and Cheddar Cheese Cubes		○	✳			○	○			○
Onion and Egg Tartlets	○	✳	●		○	●	○			○
Spinach 'Figura di Otto'		○	○			○	✳			○
Trinary Pie		○	●			✳	○			○
Vegetable Patch(work) Tart		●		✳	●	●	○			
Vegetable Wellington			●	●	✳	●	○			
Meat & Fish										
Chicken, Chorizo and Spinach Pie		○	●			✳	○			
Cod and Salsa with Puff Pastry Tacos				●	✳					●
Crab and Fennel Vol-au-vents	○	○	○	●	✳	○	○			●
Crispy Prawns, Sweet and Sour							✳			
My Mum's 'Tatty Pot' Pie			✳			●				
Oxtail Scrunch Pot Pie	○	○	○	○	○	○	✳			○
Sausage and Fig Plait			●	●	●	●	○			✳
Slow-Braised Pork Cheek and Mushroom Pie	○		✳	○	○	●	○			○
Suitably Kooky Fish Pie		✳	●			●				
Crunch & Crumb										
Arlettes				✳	●					
Croissant Cubes										✳
Mini Beignets	✳									
Raspberry Straws				●	✳					
Seeded Crackers							✳			
Strudel Scrunches							✳			
Tear and Dunk Viennoiserie Loaf										✳

CHAPTER 2

Fruit

ROASTED RHUBARB AND RASPBERRY TART

Fruit tarts are so delicious yet simple, really. Pastry, custard, fruit... that's it. I never feel the need to glaze the fruit as the natural flavours and vibrant colours are splendid enough as they are. The arrangement of the fruit is what gives this tart the wow factor, and for that reason they are among my favourite things to make. I can faff about for ages... creating a beautiful fruit topping, adding texture with pastry shapes and bursts of fresh flavour with herbs and edible flowers. I have used a selection of summer fruits here, but really you can use anything you like, depending on season, availability and personal preference.

SERVES 6,

using a rectangular, fluted loose-bottomed tart tin measuring 30 x 12 x 2.5cm (12 x 4½ x 1in)

1 quantity Sweet Shortcrust pastry (see page 12)

For the crème pâtissière
4 egg yolks
85g (3oz/7 tablespoons) caster (superfine) sugar
60g (2oz/scant ½ cup) plain (all-purpose) flour
330ml (11fl oz/1½ cups minus 1 tablespoon) milk
1 teaspoon vanilla bean paste

For the rhubarb
200g (7oz) rhubarb
75g (2¾oz/6 tablespoons) caster (superfine) sugar
aromatic spices, star anise and cardamom work well (optional)
juice of 1 clementine, or 50ml (1⅔fl oz/3½ tablespoons) water

Fruit
raspberries
red-fleshed plums
baby figs
cherries
blueberries
black seedless grapes

To finish
baked pastry shapes (optional)
Greek basil (optional)
edible flowers (optional)

ALTERNATIVE & CREATIVE PASTRY

● GF | VE
○ CH | P | SH | VIE

Make the pastry following the recipe on page 12. After resting, line, blind bake and trim a pastry case using the tips and method on page 38. Any spare pastry can be cut into shapes, baked separately and added to the tart for extra decoration.

Make the crème pâtissière by adding the egg yolks and one-third of the sugar to a large bowl. Whisk until the yolks are pale and have some volume, then add the flour, whisking to combine. In a large saucepan, bring the milk, the remaining sugar and the vanilla to the boil, removing from the heat as soon as it does. Pour a little of the hot milk over the egg yolk mixture, whisking continuously, then add the remainder. Pour the custard back into the pan and bring to a gentle boil again. Allow the custard to bubble and thicken for about 2 minutes, whisking throughout. Once thickened, remove from the pan and place in a bowl, covering the surface with a layer of cling film before it cools, to prevent a skin forming. Allow to cool completely, then keep in the fridge until needed.

Preheat the oven to 180°C (350°F), Gas Mark 4. Cut the rhubarb into long pieces, so they fit into a roasting tray. Toss with the sugar and add some spices, if desired, then squeeze over the clementine juice or pour over the water. Roast in the oven for 15–20 minutes, depending on the thickness of the stems. When tender yet still intact, remove the rhubarb from the tray to a plate lined with a clean tea towel and allow to cool. Discard the spices, if used. Once cool, cut into bite-size pieces and place to one side.

Wash and prepare the other fruit – varying how you slice each will add interest and texture to the finished tart.

Whisk the cooled crème pâtissière vigorously until smooth, then spoon a generous layer over the prepared pastry case, levelling it off. Start placing the fruit over the custard, being decorative and creative in the design, until it has been completely covered. Tuck any baked pastry pieces that may have been made in and around the tart, then add extra little dots of crème pâtissière to highlight the design. Finish with some Greek basil leaves and edible flowers, if you like, remembering that these are added for their flavour, not just for décor. Here I have used a variety of Phlox flowers and Salvia 'Hot Lips', along with some white Forget-me-nots.

Best served at room temperature.

POACHED PEACH, ZABAGLIONE AND SWEET STRUDEL SCRUNCH

I've tried to keep this recipe as simple as possible, as there is such joy in eating a perfect peach mid-summer – to mess around too much would be a travesty and a waste of a peach. Other stone fruits could be used if white peaches are unavailable.

Drying the shaped strudel pastry for up to 12 hours prior to baking is highly advantageous, so do factor this into your timings.

SERVES 6

1 quantity Sheet pastry (see page 30)

For the peaches
3 white-fleshed peaches (ripe but not soft)
200g (7oz/1 cup) caster sugar
500ml (17fl oz/2 cups plus 2 tablespoons) water
1 teaspoon vanilla bean paste

For the coulis
60g (2¼oz) raspberries

For the zabaglione
4 egg yolks
4 tablespoons caster (superfine) sugar
4 tablespoons dessert wine, such as Muscat

To finish
whole raspberries
edible flowers (optional)
icing (powdered) sugar

Make, stretch and trim the sheet pastry following the recipe on page 30, then make the strudel scrunches on page 187. Before baking, allow these to dry at room temperature for a minimum of 4 hours, then bake them as close to assembling the dessert as possible – they are best when freshly baked.

Cut each peach along and around their natural seam, then gently twist each half in opposite directions until the halves separate. If the stones are hard to remove, leave in until after poaching.

To make the poaching syrup, place the sugar, water and vanilla in a saucepan over a medium heat and stir until the sugar has dissolved, then heat the liquid until just simmering. Place the peach halves in the syrup, cut-side down, then cover with a piece of non-stick baking paper. Poach the peaches for 4 minutes with the pan set on the lowest heat. Carefully turn the peaches, cover again and poach for a further 2 minutes. The peaches should be soft but not mushy – if the peaches are softening quickly, adjust the poaching time accordingly.

Remove the fruit from the syrup using a slotted spoon, reserving the liquid, and allow everything to cool. When the peaches are cool to the touch, gently remove the skin, which should come away with ease. Any stones left in should now also be easily removed.

For the coulis, blitz the raspberries with 50ml (2fl oz) of the reserved poaching syrup. Pass through a sieve, discard the pips and set to one side.

Preheat the oven to 180ºC (350ºF), Gas Mark 4. Bake the prepared strudel scrunches in the oven for 5 minutes, after which time take a look at them. The pastry will cook and colour quickly because of how fine and dry it is, however, a few more minutes may be required to achieve a lovely golden hue – be vigilant after the 5-minute point. When done, remove from the oven, lift out of their tins and set on a wire rack.

To make the zabaglione, place the egg yolks, sugar and wine in a heatproof bowl. Whisk everything together, then set the bowl on top of a saucepan of simmering water, but without the base of the bowl touching the water. Continue to whisk and do so continuously until the heat from the steam below cooks the eggs. To prevent the mixture overheating, remove the bowl from the pan momentarily every so often. Whisk for 10 minutes until the zabaglione has quadrupled in size – an electric hand whisk would speed up the process.

Divide the coulis among the serving glasses and add in some raspberries. Top with a peach half, a drizzle of the remaining poaching syrup and a generous amount of zabaglione. Choose an edible flower with a flavour that complements the dessert – here I have used Mimulus. Dust the strudel scrunches with icing sugar and serve alongside the prepared desserts.

APPLE ROSE TART (2020)

I have been arranging and baking these tarts since the apple rose phenomenon first burst onto social media a few years back – I don't think I'll ever tire of making them. Each and every one is unique, as the mood upon making is captured within the arrangement of the apples, a bit like a painting. Granted, these tarts take a bit of effort and, yes, they are pretty, but most importantly, they taste great. It would be a real shame to spend a lot of time making something look this special if the taste and texture didn't match up.

SERVES 9,
using a 22 x 2.5cm (8½ x 1in) square,
fluted loose-bottomed tart tin

1 quantity Sweet Shortcrust pastry (see page 12)

For the frangipane
75g (2¾oz/⅓ cup) unsalted butter, at room temperature
75g (2¾oz/6 tablespoons) caster (superfine) sugar
35g (1¼oz) ground hazelnuts
40g (1½oz) ground almonds
75g (2¾oz) eggs (shelled weight), lightly beaten

For the apples
juice of 2 large lemons
12 dessert apples, a mixture in variety and skin colour
100ml (3½fl oz/⅓ cup plus 1 tablespoon) water
50g (1¾oz/¼ cup) caster (superfine) sugar
½ teaspoon ground cinnamon

To finish
blueberries and cherries, halved (optional)
1 egg yolk
boiling water
caster (superfine) sugar
icing (powdered) sugar

ALTERNATIVE & CREATIVE PASTRY

● GF

Make the pastry following the recipe on page 12. After resting, line, blind bake and trim a pastry case, using the tips and techniques on page 38. Leave the baked case within the tin for later. Any spare pastry can be cut into shapes and used to make decorative flourishes later.

To make the frangipane, place the soft butter into the bowl of a freestanding mixer along with the caster (superfine) sugar. Attach the paddle and beat for 1 minute until creamed. Add the nuts and eggs alternately in 3 consecutive bursts, beating continuously between additions. When all of the ingredients are well combined, spread the frangipane evenly across the prepared pastry case. Set aside.

Next, start on the apples. Half-fill a medium saucepan with water and squeeze in the juice of 1 lemon. Bring to a gentle simmer. Add the juice of the other lemon to a bowl of cold water. Core four of the apples and cut them in half vertically. Slice each apple half across its width to 1mm (or as thinly as possible) – using a mandolin will give consistently even slices.

Submerge the slices in the simmering water for a few minutes to soften, testing after 1 minute and every 30 seconds thereafter. To test, bend and roll a slice between your fingers, if it cracks, wait another 30 seconds, then re-test. When ready, the slices will be soft and pliable. Transfer to the cold water using a slotted spoon.

To make a rose, use up to eight slices of apple at one time. Lay onto a tea towel, skin facing upwards, laying left to right and overlapping each slice by half. Roll up starting at the left-hand side, gently working the apple slices into a complete roll. Place into the frangipane, then ease open to create the look of a blooming rose. When all of the apple slices have been used, repeat the slicing and softening process with another batch of apples, and repeat until enough roses have been made to cover the surface. Any gaps can be filled with single apple slices tightly rolled in between and, if using, additional fruits can be added, too, as can pastry shapes.

When finished decorating, make the syrup by first boiling the water, sugar and ground cinnamon together until reduced and thickened. Allow to cool for 5 minutes, then carefully brush over the apple flesh. Place in the fridge for at least an hour.

Place a baking sheet in the oven and preheat to 160°C (325°F), Gas Mark 3. If pastry décor has been used, brush the pastry carefully with egg wash (see page 38). Sprinkle the tart with a fine dusting of caster (superfine) sugar, cover with kitchen foil and place in the oven. Baking the tart under foil can take up to 2 hours, but it is worth it, as the colour of the fruit will hold better and the flavour will intensify significantly. Check the tart after 1 hour, then every 20 minutes thereafter, removing the foil for the final 20 minutes of baking.

Allow to cool for 15 minutes before removing from the tin and slicing. Dust with a little icing (powdered) sugar and serve with or without cream.

APRICOT AND VANILLA DANISH
WITH FENNEL SEED CARAMEL

Aniseed is such a distinct flavour note and one that is found naturally in many different ingredients – think tarragon, star anise, liquorice and fennel. I use all of these ingredients often, in both sweet and savoury dishes, to add depth of flavour and an edge of curiosity. It's fennel seeds that provide the aniseed note here – when added to a sweet caramel and paired with sharp yet nectarous apricots, the flavour once again proves to be a very pleasing and perhaps surprising seasoning.

MAKES 6 PASTRIES

1 quantity Viennoiserie pastry (see page 26)

For the crème pâtissière
3 egg yolks
60g (2oz/5 tablespoons) caster (superfine) sugar
20g (¾oz/2⅓ tablespoons) plain (all-purpose) flour
10g (⅓oz/1 tablespoon plus 2 teaspoons) cornflour (cornstarch)
250ml (8½fl oz/1 cup plus 1 tablespoon) milk
1 teaspoon vanilla bean paste

For the apricots
3 firm but ripe apricots (if in season – if not, plums are a good alternative)
200g (7oz) water
100g (3½oz/½ cup) caster (superfine) sugar
½ teaspoon vanilla bean paste

For the fennel seed caramel
50g (1¾oz/¼ cup) caster (superfine) sugar
100ml (3½fl oz/⅓ cup plus 1 tablespoon) water
1 tablespoon fennel seeds

To finish
egg wash (see page 38)
icing (powdered) sugar
fennel or dill flowers or fronds (optional)

ALTERNATIVE & CREATIVE PASTRY

● IP | P
○ CH | GF | SH | SW

Make the Viennoiserie pastry following the recipe on page 26. While proving and folding, prepare the fillings.

To make the crème pâtissière, follow the method on page 48, adding the cornflour (cornstarch) at the same time as the flour.

To poach the apricots, carefully halve and de-stone each. Mix together the water, sugar and vanilla to make a poaching liquid. Gently heat, stirring, until the sugar has dissolved and the liquid is syrupy. Add the apricots and turn the heat to the lowest setting, poaching the fruit up to for 5 minutes, turning them halfway through. Remove the pan from the heat but allow the apricots to cool in the syrup. Transfer to a bowl and store in the fridge.

To make the caramel, place the sugar and water in a frying pan and set over a medium heat. When the sugar has dissolved, keep a close eye on the liquid, but do not stir. As the sugar starts to caramelize and turn amber, swirl the pan around so that it cooks evenly. When a medium amber colour has been reached, sprinkle in the fennel seeds and immediately pour the caramel onto a silicone mat or non-stick baking paper. Allow to cool and set, then break into small shards.

When the dough has had the final fold and is rested, roll out (see page 28) and cut into 6 squares, each measuring 11x 11cm (4¼ x 4½in). Don't throw away any scraps (see page 191). Lay on a baking sheet lined with non-stick baking paper with sufficient gaps between each to allow for expansion then fold each square in half to form a triangle. Turn each triangle so that the base is facing you, then use a sharp knife to make incisions along the two sides, starting 1cm from the edge. It is important that the incisions don't quite meet at the top, as this will hold the pastry together once folded. Unfold the triangle then cross each cut piece over the other to create a pocket, lining up all points as best you can.

I blind bake these pastries, adding the fillings afterwards. Wrap a small handful of baking beans in ovenproof cling film and layer it by three. Set in the middle of each pastry, then cover loosely with cling film and prove for up to 3 hours (see timeline on page 28).

When ready to bake, preheat the oven to 180°C (350°F), Gas Mark 4. Brush the smooth surfaces of each pastry with egg wash, being careful not to let any drip onto the layers. Bake in the oven for 20–25 minutes (with the weights still in place), or until dark golden. Don't be tempted to take the pastries out too early – the longer bake will ensure the crunch and the delicious flakiness that is so desirable.

Cool on wire racks, removing the weights, then when cold, pipe in some of the crème pâtissière, add an apricot half, some of the fennel caramel and finish with a dusting of icing (powdered) sugar. Decorate with fennel or dill flowers or fronds, if using, and eat cold.

APPLE TARTE TATIN

Apple tarte tatin is a thing of pure joy when done right. Twice-baking the apples, a method I learnt from Raymond Blanc's *Kitchen Secrets*, is the real secret to success – that and the use of homemade puff pastry. The pastry blanket will soak up some of the viscous apple juice and the bubbling amber caramel will colour the apples beautifully. This dessert will wow, it will engrave itself on your memory, and you will make it time and time again, I'm sure.

MAKES 1 TART TO SERVE 6,
using a 20 x 5cm (8 x 2in) tarte tatin dish

1 quantity Puff pastry (see page 16)
egg wash (see page 38)

For the apples
8 dessert apples – Cox's work well
1 teaspoon vanilla bean paste (optional)
30g (1oz/2 tablespoons) unsalted butter, melted

For the caramel
100g (3½oz/½ cup) caster (superfine) sugar
50ml (1⅔fl oz/3½ tablespoons) water
50g (1¾oz/3½ tablespoon) unsalted butter, cut into 1cm (½in) cubes

ALTERNATIVE & CREATIVE PASTRY

● GF | IP | SH | SW

Make and prepare the puff pastry using the recipe and method on page 16. After the final fold, rest in the fridge for at least 1 hour. If the pastry has been made in advance, see notes on page 19 prior to rolling.

Roll out the puff pastry to approximately 3mm (⅛in) depth and cut a circle from it, 1cm (½in) larger than the baking dish being used. Rest the pastry upon a baking tray lined with non-stick baking paper and place back into the fridge for later. Do save the remaining pastry for another use.

Snugly line the base of the tarte tatin dish with a circle of non-stick baking paper. Preheat the oven to 180°C (350°F), Gas Mark 4.

Peel, core and quarter the apples, rounding off each sharp edge (for a tighter fit), then set to one side while making the caramel. Add the sugar and water to a frying pan, stirring until the sugar dissolves, then place over a medium heat and allow to bubble. As the caramel cooks, do not stir, instead swirl the pan so the parts that are colouring first mix into the liquid, allowing the caramel to colour evenly. When light-amber bubbles appear, start to add the cubed butter a little at a time, whisking between each addition. When all of the butter has been added, pour into the paper-lined baking dish. Leave to cool for a few minutes, then neatly arrange the apples around the dish, working from the outside in.

Mix the vanilla paste with the melted butter in a small bowl and brush the exposed apple flesh with it. Bake in the oven for 30 minutes, then remove and allow to cool. Both the apples and the dish need to be cooled sufficiently before adding the pastry to avoid it melting upon contact. Collect the pastry from the fridge and place it on top of the fruit. Tuck the pastry between the apples and the dish's side, using the back of a spoon.

Brush the surface of the pastry with the egg wash. Pierce the pastry once, making a small steam hole. Place back into the oven for up to 40 minutes – until the pastry has risen and the dish shows signs of sticky caramel bubbling up its sides.

When done, remove from the oven and allow to cool for at least 10 minutes before inverting onto a plate. Remove the paper disc, slice and serve warm.

Ice cream complements this perfectly.

LYCHEE AND VIOLET CRAQUELIN CHOUX

I created this recipe with my mum in mind, a beautiful soul whom I love so dearly. When Mum first became ill with an aggressive form of dementia, she was frightened, paralysed with anxiety and fell into a deep depression. She both gave up on and forgot about all the foods she once loved. She lost 4½ stone – it was such a sad and worrying thing to witness. It was a can of lychees that saved her, a random find at the back of her cupboard that we desperately tried to offer her. She loved the sweet floral syrup, the soft and easily digested flesh of the fruit. She ate nothing else for weeks, until her appetite returned, the depression lifted and she learned once again to enjoy her food.

MAKES APPROXIMATELY 16 SMALL CHOUX BUNS

1 quantity Choux pastry (see page 24)

For the crème pâtissière
6 egg yolks
120g (4oz/⅔ cup minus 2 teaspoons) caster (superfine) sugar
40g (1½oz/3¼ tablespoons) plain (all-purpose) flour
20g (⅔oz/2 tablespoons plus 4 teaspoons) cornflour (cornstarch)
400ml (14fl oz/1⅔ cup) milk
50g (1¾oz) parma violet sweets, crushed to powder
100ml (3⅓ fl oz/⅓ cup plus 1 tablespoon) lychee syrup (reserved from the tin)
purple or pink food colouring (optional)

For the craquelin
50g (1¾oz/3½ tablespoons) unsalted butter, softened
50g (1¾oz/¼ cup) caster (superfine) sugar
50g (1¾oz/⅓ cup) plain (all-purpose) flour

For the fruit layer
1 x 425g tin of lychees, drained, juice reserved
violet liqueur (optional)

To finish (all optional)
edible silver dust or icing (powdered) sugar
white chocolate buttons
edible flowers

ALTERNATIVE & CREATIVE PASTRY

○ GF | IP | P | SH | SW | VIE

First make the crème pâtissière, following the method on page 48, adding the parma violets and the lychee syrup to the milk and sugar. Once thickened, transfer to a bowl, whisk in a few drops of food colouring (if using) then cover the surface with clingfilm and allow to cool completely. Keep in the fridge until needed.

To make the craquelin, simply mix all of the ingredients together to form a paste – you can either do this by hand or use a mixer. Spread the paste on one sheet of non-stick baking paper and cover with another, then roll out to 1mm (or as thinly as possible) thick. Place this in the freezer, paper and all, for at least 30 minutes.

Preheat the oven to 180°C (350°F), Gas Mark 4. Make the pastry following the recipe on page 24, then transfer to a piping bag fitted with a plain 2cm (¾in) nozzle. Allow to cool for 20 minutes. Onto two pieces of non-stick baking paper set on baking sheets, pipe out 16 rounds of choux pastry, each measuring approximately 3.5cm (1½in) in diameter and 1.5cm (¾in) in height. If you want to be super consistent in size, draw around a circular pastry cutter and use these markings as a template when piping, but do remember to turn the sheet of paper over before piping to avoid the pen ink transferring to the baked choux.

Remove the craquelin from the freezer and cut circles from it using a 4cm (1½in) round pastry cutter. Lay one craquelin disc on top of each choux.

Bake in the oven for 20 minutes, then reduce the heat to 140°C (275°F), Gas Mark 1 and bake for a further 20 minutes. It is really important that the oven door remains closed until the full baking time is complete. After the total 40 minutes, remove from the oven and pierce the bottom of each bun with a skewer, to allow the steam to escape. Transfer to a wire rack to cool.

Drain and dry the lychees well, finely chop the fruit and add to a bowl with a splash of violet liqueur, if using.

Remove the crème pâtissière from the fridge and whisk vigorously until smooth, then transfer to a piping bag fitted with a 2cm (¾in) star-shaped piping nozzle.

Carefully slice the top third off each baked choux bun. Into the bottom part of each bun, pipe enough crème pâtissière to cover the base of the pastry. Spoon in some of the lychees and then decoratively pipe some more crème pâtissière on top. Replace the choux hat and, if you like, shower with silver dust (or icing (powdered) sugar), decorate with white chocolate buttons and some edible flowers – here I have used fairy pansies and forget-me-nots.

BOOZY CHERRY LIQUOR PIE

Cherry brandy isn't particularly in vogue these days. I recently asked for some on the rocks (trying and failing to be cool) in a rather trendy bar in London. I was faced with an astonished look; they clearly didn't stock cherry brandy and obviously weren't asked for it very often! But I love it – that retro appeal, the sticky and heady alcoholic sweetness – and it's a great digestive with which I've ended many a special night. As it turns out, it is also very good when used in a pie.

SERVES 9–12,
using a loose-bottomed 20 x 3.5cm (8 x 1½in) square tin

2 quantities Sweet Shortcrust pastry (see page 12)

For the filling
1kg (35oz) frozen dark sweet cherries, stoned
120g (4oz/⅔ cup minus 2 teaspoons) caster (superfine) sugar
3 tablespoons cornflour (cornstarch), mixed with 2 tablespoons cold water
30g (1oz/2 tablespoons) unsalted butter
120ml (4fl oz/½ cup) cherry brandy
½ teaspoon vanilla bean paste
½ teaspoon almond extract

To finish
egg wash (see page 38)
caster (superfine) sugar, for sprinkling (optional)
edible flowers (optional)
crème fraîche, to serve

ALTERNATIVE & CREATIVE PASTRY

● VE
○ CH | GF | P | SH | VIE

Make the pastry following the recipe on page 12. Using one half of the rested pastry, line, blind bake and trim a pastry case (see tips and techniques on page 38), leaving it in the tin for later. The remaining pastry will be used to create the pie lid. Keep this wrapped in cling film, and return to the fridge while preparing the filling.

Place the cherries and sugar in a saucepan and heat over a low setting for 10 minutes. The juice from the fruit will soon ooze out. Add the cornflour (cornstarch) paste, increase the heat and allow to boil, stirring, then reduce to a simmer and cook until thickened.

Strain the cherries through a colander, returning the juice to the pan to be reduced and thickened further. Tip the cherries into a bowl for later. Add the butter to the cherry juice and stir well; simmer for up to 30 minutes to reduce the liquid. Turn off the heat, allow to cool, then stir the reduced liquid into the cherries along with the cherry brandy, vanilla paste and almond extract. Chill in the fridge for at least an hour.

Fill the prepared pastry case with the chilled filling and use the remaining pastry to create the pie lid, whether covering with a decorative top (as pictured) or leaving plain, refer to the notes on page 42 for how to transfer the lid to the base successfully.

Preheat the oven to 180°C (350°F), Gas Mark 4. Evenly brush the surface of the pie with the egg wash. If the décor is intricate, an artist's brush would be the tool of choice. When done, give the pie an even yet generous sprinkling of caster (superfine) sugar (if using) and place in the oven for up to 1 hour, checking it a couple of times during baking – if any decorative parts are browning too quickly, cover these with kitchen foil.

Remove from the oven and allow to cool for at least 15 minutes before removing from the tin and slicing.

If finishing with edible flowers, it is important to think about their flavour and not use them solely for decoration. I have used Salvia 'Hot Lips' here – the flavour pop works beautifully with the cherry filling. Remember to remove any green parts before eating.

Serve warm with a generous dollop of crème fraîche.

SALTED CARAMEL BANANA TARTE TATINS

Salted caramel with baked bananas is a match made in heaven. The sweetness and flavour of the fruit intensifies during baking and the salt balances that perfectly. My advice is to make these into mini tarte tatins, those not meant for sharing (upon tasting you'll understand why!), I very much doubt you'll want to share yours either.

MAKES 4 TARTE TATINS,
using mini tarte tatin tins measuring 10 x
   2.5cm (4 x 1in)

1 quantity Puff pastry (see page 16)
plain (all-purpose) flour, for dusting
3–4 firm, not too ripe, bananas, peeled
egg wash (see page 38)

For the salted caramel
150g (5⅓oz/¾ cup) caster (superfine) sugar
100ml (3⅓fl oz/⅓ cup plus 1 tablespoon)
   water
½ teaspoon vanilla bean paste
50g (1¾oz/3½ tablespoons) unsalted butter,
   cut into 1cm (½in) cubes
pinch of Maldon salt flakes

ALTERNATIVE & CREATIVE PASTRY

● GF | IP | SH | SW

Make the pastry following the recipe on page 16. After the final fold, rest the pastry in the fridge for at least 1 hour. If you have made this further in advance, see the notes on page 19. On a lightly floured surface, roll the puff pastry to 5mm (¼in) depth. Cut out four circles, 1cm (½in) larger than the tins being used. Rest on non-stick baking paper, then place on a baking tray and put in the fridge for later. Save any extra pastry for another use.

Cut four circles of non-stick baking paper to tightly fit the bottom of each tarte tatin tin and set inside.

Cut the bananas into 3mm (⅛in) slices, using a mandolin if you want to be precise – I then cut circles from each slice of banana using the reverse of a piping nozzle, but this isn't essential, it just gives a nice even finish. Set the prepared bananas to one side.

To make the caramel, place the sugar, water and vanilla in a frying pan and set over a medium heat. When the sugar has dissolved, keep a close eye on the liquid, but do not stir. As the sugar starts to caramelize and turn amber, swirl the contents of the pan around so that it cooks evenly. When light-amber bubbles start to pop, add the butter – a little at a time – whisking between each addition. Add a little Maldon salt, give it one final whisk, then divide the caramel among the paper-lined tins. Leave to cool for a few minutes, then neatly arrange the prepared banana slices snugly around the tins, working from the inside out. Add a second layer of

bananas to any part that needs levelling off – there's no need to be neat this time, these slices won't show when each tart is flipped.

Preheat the oven to 180°C (350°F), Gas Mark 4. Remove the pastry discs from the fridge and put one of these on top of each of the banana tarts, tucking the edges into the tins with the back of a spoon or similar.

Brush the surface of the pastry with the egg wash. Add a small steam hole to each lid, place the tarts on a baking tray and bake in the oven for 30 minutes, or until the pastry has risen and the sides of the tins are bubbling with caramel.

Remove from the oven, allow to cool for 10 minutes, then invert each onto a serving plate. Remove the paper discs, sprinkle the tops with some extra salt flakes and serve warm, perhaps with ice cream.

MANGO AND COCONUT CREAM TARTLETS

There is great appeal in dainty things, and beautifully prepared petit fours make no exception. These tiny tarts would work well at a party or served as part of an afternoon tea. You can change the fruits if you like – most will work well nestled atop the coconut cream.

I suggest using the Vegan pastry on page 34 to make these tart shells, as the coconut oil used in the pastry complements the filling perfectly. For an all-vegan version, simply substitute the cream cheese with a coconut-based alternative.

MAKES 40 PETIT FOURS,
using specialist petit fours tins

½ quantity Sweet Vegan pastry (see page 34)

For the filling
100g (3½oz) cream cheese, at room temperature
50ml (1²/₃fl oz/3½ tablespoons) coconut milk
20g (⅔oz/2¼ tablespoons) icing (powdered) sugar, sifted
½ teaspoon vanilla bean paste

For the fruit layer
1 ripe mango, peeled, stoned and finely diced
pulp of 1 passion fruit
juice of 1 small lime
black seedless grapes, thinly sliced
coriander flowers and micro leaves (optional)

ALTERNATIVE & CREATIVE PASTRY

● GF | SW
○ CH | P | SH | VIE

Make the pastry following the recipe on page 34. After resting, line the petit fours tins. As the tins are so small, the pastry will need to be rolled as thinly as possible – the easiest way to do this, I find, is to use a pasta machine (see page 36), rolling through a thin setting. Cut circles from the pastry using a round cutter slightly larger than the moulds. Ease the pastry into the moulds, then cut the excess by turning each over and pushing down onto the work surface, which will trim the excess pastry, leaving a neat and tidy edge.

For blind baking, cut squares of kitchen foil a little bigger than each tin. Cover the pastry with it and manipulate the foil into the base and sides of each. Fill the foil-topped pastry cases with dried rice or lentils, place on a baking tray and chill in the fridge for 15 minutes.

Preheat the oven to 180°C (350°F), Gas Mark 4, then bake the tartlets for 5 minutes only, after which time lift and remove the rice and foil, then prick the base of each case with a fork. Return to the oven, uncovered, for 5 minutes more. As the pastry is thin and the surface area so small, they will bake very quickly and can burn easily, so be vigilant. When done, remove from the tins and transfer to a wire rack to cool. Store safely in an airtight container until needed.

To make the filling, simply whip together the cream cheese, coconut milk, icing (powdered) sugar and vanilla to a yoghurt-like consistency. Transfer to a piping bag and leave in the fridge until needed.

Place the mango in a bowl with the passion fruit pulp and squeeze in the lime juice, mixing well. Half-fill each of the prepared pastry cases with the coconut cream, then top each with some fruit. Add some sliced grapes, a coriander flower, micro leaf or both to each (if using). This not only adds décor, but the flavour works beautifully with the fruits. Finish by highlighting each tartlet with tiny dots of any remaining coconut cream.

Arrange on a platter and serve immediately.

David Austen Roses from Maddocks Farm

RASPBERRY AND ROSE GIN MILLE FEUILLE

I first came across Tinkture Rose Gin through Instagram. A foodie friend recommended it and so I tried. I was blown away by the delicate floral flavour, the rose-pink colour change when the mixer was added, the carefully designed packaging and the thoughtful ethos that was behind the production. I am a huge fan, and now Hannah, the lady behind the brand, and I are friends. To honour this new-found friendship and to celebrate this magnificent gin, I have created a recipe that will partner perfectly with a rose gin cocktail to make a special end to a celebratory meal.

This dessert does take time, so a bit of forward planning is needed – in particular, the jelly requires overnight setting. You could also make, roll and cut the pastry in advance, ready to be baked on the day.

There will be leftover jelly and mousse, as it is difficult to make both on a smaller scale. However, both can be eaten separately later – perhaps with a bowl of fruit. Slurping on leftover gin jelly will never be a sad thing, but do remember that it is extremely boozy!

MAKES 6

1 quantity Inverted Puff pastry (see page 20)
plain (all-purpose) flour, for dusting
icing (powdered) sugar, for baking

For the jelly
5 sheets gelatine (I use Dr Oetker)
150ml (5fl oz/⅔ cup) pear cordial, mixed
  with 350ml (12¼fl oz/1½ cups) water
250g (8¾oz/1¼ cups) caster (superfine)
  sugar
250ml (8½fl oz/1 cup plus 1 tablespoon)
  Tinkture Rose Gin

For the raspberry mousse
3 sheets gelatine
200g (7oz/2 cups) fresh or frozen
  raspberries, thawed if frozen
25g (¾oz/2¾ tablespoons) icing (powdered)
  sugar, plus extra for dusting
2 eggs, separated
40g (1½oz/3¼ tablespoons) caster
  (superfine) sugar
300ml (10½fl oz/1¼ cups) double (heavy)
  cream
30ml (1fl oz/2 tablespoons) pear cordial

To decorate
crystallized rose petals (optional)

ALTERNATIVE & CREATIVE PASTRY

● GF | P | SW
○ CH | SH | VIE

Make, fold and rest the pastry following the recipe on page 20. Roll between two sheets of baking paper to approximately 5mm (¼in). If, however, the pastry has been made in advance, please see the notes on page 19 prior to rolling.

The secret to achieving consistent, perfectly baked pastry ovals is rolling them all to the exact same thickness. To do this, I roll the cut pastry through a pasta machine – set to the widest setting. The pastry does have to be chilled yet pliable to do this, so as not to disrupt the buttery layers created during the folding process, so please do this with caution, or even leave out this stage if you are not too fussed about variations during baking.

First roll the pastry between the baking paper to 5mm (¼in) using a rolling pin, then, if wanting to roll through a pasta machine, cut into long, wide strips and pass through the machine, on the widest setting. Cut 18 ovals using a cutter measuring 8.5cm x 5.5cm (3½in x 2¼in), then rest in the fridge for at least 30 minutes, covering with cling film to prevent drying.

Preheat the oven to 180°C (350°F), Gas Mark 4. Depending on how many flat baking sheets are to hand, the baking of the pastry may need to be done in stages. Sift some icing (powdered) sugar onto a work surface and lay the cut pastry shapes onto it, coating one side completely. Transfer to a flat baking sheet lined with non-stick baking paper, leaving a gap between each. Top with another sheet of non-stick baking paper and lay another baking sheet on top. Place in the oven and bake for 20 minutes, after which time the pastry should be crisp and deep golden, the icing (powdered) sugar caramelized and crisp. Transfer to a wire rack and repeat until all of the pastry pieces have been baked. Allow to cool completely and then store in an airtight container until ready to assemble the desserts.

Line a 3cm (1¼in) deep baking tray that measures 30cm x 22cm (12in x 8½in) with cling film.

To make the jelly, first soak the gelatine in cold water and set to one side until softened. Make up the cordial and place it in a saucepan with the caster (superfine) sugar. Gently heat until the sugar dissolves, then add the gin.

Continued overleaf

Continued text

Remove from the heat, drain the softened gelatine and pat dry with some kitchen paper, then add to the hot gin mixture and stir until dissolved. Pour the liquid through a sieve into the pre-lined baking tray, allow to cool, then transfer to the fridge to fully set – due to the alcohol content, this should be done overnight.

For the mousse, soak the gelatine in cold water to soften. Meanwhile, blitz the raspberries in a food processor, along with the icing (powdered) sugar. Pass the fruit through a sieve, discarding the pips. Place the egg yolks in a bowl with the caster (superfine) sugar and whisk (by hand or machine) until thickened, lightened in colour and increased in volume, which should take a good 5 minutes, or longer if whisking by hand.

In a clean bowl, whisk the egg whites until white and frothy. Whip the cream to soft peaks in another bowl. Drain the softened gelatine and pat dry with some kitchen paper, then place in a small saucepan with the pear cordial and very gently heat until the gelatine dissolves. Pour the liquified gelatine into the raspberry purée and add this to the whisked egg yolks. Add one-third of the egg whites and stir in – no need to be gentle. When combined, add the remaining egg whites and the whipped cream and now gently fold everything together, preventing the egg whites from deflating and the cream from stiffening. Transfer to a piping bag fitted with a 1cm (½in) plain piping nozzle and put in the fridge. The mousse will be perfectly set after 1½

hours but can still be piped after that time, too.

Take both the set jelly and mousse from the fridge. Pipe some raspberry mousse onto six of the pastry ovals. Using the same cutter that was used for the pastry, cut six pieces of jelly (freezing for 30 minutes prior to cutting will help). Top the remaining ovals with the jelly and use those to top the mousse. Top with the last pastry ovals and decorate with some crystallized rose petals, if using. If preferred, mix and match the way in which these desserts are assembled, as shown in the image overleaf.

Serve immediately.

GLUTEN-FREE LEMON MERINGUE PIE

Making a lemon meringue pie using gluten-free pastry was a challenge – the pastry itself was a labour of love, and after finally getting that part right, I discovered the pre-baked pastry altered considerably when filled with the lemon custard, which took me back to square one. With some final tweaks and a slight compromize on the texture of the lemon layer, this pie has everything a standard gluten-based lemon meringue pie has – crisp, delicious pastry, a tart and creamy filling, and a crunchy yet soft-centred meringue top.

As you're not creating a pie lid there is enough pastry to make two cases. I have doubled the fillings and toppings, so this recipe makes two pies – one for you and one for a friend!

MAKES 2 PIES, EACH SERVING 6,
using two deep, fluted, loose-bottomed
** 18 x 3cm (7 x 1¼in) circular tart tins**

1 quantity Sweet Gluten-free Pastry (see page 32)
cornflour (cornstarch), for dusting

For the filling
100g (3½oz/½ cup) caster (superfine) sugar
60g (2oz/½ cup) cornflour (cornstarch)
juice of 4–5 lemons – 180ml (6¼fl oz) in total
6 egg yolks (save the whites for the meringue topping)
450ml (15fl oz/1¾ cups plus 1 tablespoon) double (heavy) cream

For the meringue
130g (4½oz) egg whites
250g (9oz/1¼ cups) caster (superfine) sugar
1 tablespoon cornflour (cornstarch)

Make the pastry following the recipe on page 32. After resting in the fridge, roll it out between two sheets of non-stick baking paper (a gentle dusting of cornflour might be beneficial). Blind bake two pastry cases, following the tips and techniques on page 38, however the pastry can be successfully pushed into the tin using your fingertips, if preferred.

To make the filling, place the sugar, cornflour (cornstarch) and lemon juice in a heatproof bowl and mix well. Stir in the egg yolks to combine. Heat the cream in a saucepan until it is just starting to boil, then pour a little onto the egg mixture, whisking well before slowly pouring in the remainder. Return the mixture to the pan and bring back to the boil, whisking continuously. Once boiling, reduce the heat and simmer for a minute or two. Fret not if the appearance changes, it is only a reaction between ingredients that will be rectified later. Remove from the heat and allow to cool fully.

Pour the cooled custard into a food processor and blend until smooth, then pour into the pre-baked pastry cases, levelling out with a palette knife.

Preheat the oven to 100°C (212°F), Gas Mark ¼. To make the meringue, pour the egg whites into the clean bowl of a freestanding mixer and attach the whisk. Whisk on a medium speed for a few minutes until the whites stiffen to soft peaks (test by tipping the bowl, if the egg whites slide, mix a little longer). Mix together the sugar and cornflour (cornstarch) and add this, one tablespoon at a time, to the egg whites with the whisk running continuously. When all of the sugar has been incorporated, turn the speed to low and whisk for 2 minutes more or until no sugar crystals can be felt between your fingers.

Spoon the meringue over the lemon layers, spreading it out gently across the surface. Do make sure you bring the meringue right to the very sides of the pastry cases as this creates a blanket of insulation for the creamy filling below. Push the meringue around with the back of a spoon, swooshing and swirling to create texture, then bake in the oven for 1 hour, after which time the meringue's exterior will be crisp yet the inside still soft. Switch off the oven, leaving the pies inside for 30 minutes more, without opening the oven door. Remove from the oven and allow to cool for 15 minutes before removing the tins.

Serve warm or allow to cool completely if preferred – pouring cream is optional.

CHAPTER 3

Cream & Cheese

CHAMOMILE PANNA COTTA TART

This really is a dreamy dessert – sweet, creamy and meltingly unctuous, and the pristine white surface makes the perfect canvas for artistic decoration. The panna cotta can, of course, be made without the encasing pastry but doing so would mean losing the welcoming crunch.

There will be a little of the panna cotta mix left over, which if set into a separate glass will provide a perfect gluten-free alternative dessert, should one be needed.

SERVES 8–10,
using a fluted, loose-bottomed 23 x
  3.5cm (9 x 1½in) circular tin

1 quantity Sweet Shortcrust pastry
  (see page 12)
egg wash (see page 38)

For the panna cotta
150ml (5fl oz/⅔ cup) milk
4 chamomile tea bags
4 sheets gelatine (I use Dr Oetker)
800ml (26fl oz/3¼ cups plus 1
  tablespoon) double (heavy) cream
200g (7oz/1 cup) caster (superfine) sugar

For the topping
a selection of prepared fresh fruits
baked pastry shapes
edible flowers and herbs
sugar sprinkles

ALTERNATIVE & CREATIVE PASTRY

● GF

Make and rest the pastry following the recipe on page 12, then line, blind bake and trim a pastry case, using the tips and techniques on page 38. Any leftover pastry can be cut into decorative shapes, egg-washed and baked separately to be used as extra decoration.

For the panna cotta, add the milk and tea bags to a saucepan and bring to a simmer. Once simmering, switch off the heat and allow the tea to infuse for 15 minutes. Remove the tea bags, giving them a good squeeze before discarding. Soften the gelatine by soaking the sheets in a bowl of cold water.

Add the cream and sugar to the pan of infused milk. Slowly bring the mixture to the boil, stirring now and then to dissolve the sugar. As soon as boiling point is reached, turn off the heat. Drain the softened gelatine and pat dry with kitchen paper before stirring into the hot cream. When the gelatine has fully dissolved, pass the mixture through a fine sieve into a clean bowl and allow to cool. Once cooled, place in the fridge, checking and stirring every so often until the panna cotta starts to thicken. The ideal pouring consistency required is that of thick custard.

Once thickened, carefully pour into the prepared pastry case. Any bubbles that rise to the surface can easily be popped by running the flame of a blow torch over the surface, however this isn't a necessity, it's purely for aesthetics. Place back in the fridge until fully set – this should take around 4 hours. Decorate the tart with a variety of fruits, baked pastry shapes, petals, edible flowers, sprinkles and herbs.

When ready to serve, use a hot dry knife to slice the tart perfectly, wiping the knife between slicing. Serve with an extra portion of fruit macerated with a sprinkling of caster (superfine) sugar and a splash of booze, if you like.

BUTTERSCOTCH CRUNCH WITH CRYSTALLIZED ROSEMARY

Crystallized rosemary is a complete revelation; it's really simple to make and is absolutely delicious. It pairs so well with the butterscotch here, so do make it – it elevates these bite-size treats from simple to sophisticated. The cups can successfully be made into dessert-size portions, too – just be sure to offset the extra sweetness of a larger portion with some sharp fruit or pouring cream.

MAKES 24 CUPS,
using 2 x 12-hole mini muffin mould trays

1 quantity Sheet pastry (see page 30)
50g (1¾oz/3½ tablespoons) unsalted butter, melted

For the crystallized rosemary

200g (7oz/¾ cup plus 2 tablespoons cup) caster (superfine) sugar, plus extra for rolling
100ml (3½fl oz/⅓ cup plus 1 tablespoon) water
3 sprigs of rosemary, leaves cut into bundles
rosemary or thyme flowers (optional)
other edible flowers (optional)

For the butterscotch

175g (6oz/¾ cup plus 1 teaspoon) unsalted butter
175g (6oz/¾ cup plus 2 tablespoons) soft dark brown sugar
40g (1½oz/3¼ tablespoons) plain (all-purpose) flour
200ml (6¾fl oz/¾ cup plus 2 tablespoons) double (heavy) cream
2 teaspoons vanilla bean paste
Maldon salt

ALTERNATIVE & CREATIVE PASTRY

● GF | SW
○ VIE

Make and stretch the pastry following the recipe and method on page 30, then lightly brush the entire surface with the melted butter. Allow to dry a little before cutting into 7cm (2¾in) squares. Line each tray with 3 squares of the buttered pastry per hole, alternating the direction in which they are laid, which adds a textured edge to each.

Preheat the oven to 180°C (350°F), Gas Mark 4. The easiest, most efficient way to blind bake these mini pastry cases is to lay a few layers of ovenproof cling film over the top of the trays and fill each hole with dried rice. Bake in the oven for 8 minutes, then remove the weight and cling film. Prick the base of each pastry cup with a fork and pop back into the oven for a final crisp and to gain some colour. When done, lift out of the trays onto a wire rack and allow to cool fully.

To crystallize the rosemary, add the sugar and water to a small saucepan and stir until the sugar has dissolved. Simmer until reduced by half, then add the trimmed leaves, submerging them in the syrup. Take off the heat and allow the leaves to infuse for 2 minutes. Sprinkle some sugar onto a plate, remove the rosemary leaves from the pan, shaking off any excess syrup. Toss into the sugar and shake the plate until the leaves are coated. Transfer to a sheet of non-stick baking paper to dry and harden.

To make the butterscotch, simply melt the butter and brown sugar together in a saucepan, sprinkle in the flour, pour in the milk and add the vanilla. Heat until boiling, then reduce to a simmer, stirring often, and allow to thicken – this should only take a few minutes. Pour the mixture through a sieve into a jug and fill each pastry cup with the sauce while still hot. Add a little flake of Maldon salt to each and allow to cool.

Garnish each with a sprig of crystallized rosemary and finish with edible flowers, if you like, choosing those that will complement the tartlets. Rosemary and thyme flowers will naturally work well, and the addition of Mallow flowers is not simply for aesthetics, they were chosen because of their delicate flavour.

These are best on the day of making.

VANILLA SLICES

I have childhood memories of my Nana Maud tucking into a vanilla slice. We'd go to town every Friday and that would be her treat, partnered with the strongest cup of tea I have seen anybody drink. I wish I could have made her my version; although it's very different from the ones she used to buy, I can only imagine she would approve.

The method for these may seem laborious, but rest assured the gratification upon eating is worth every moment spent making them. This is the perfect recipe to show off homemade puff pastry. The gelatine within the custard needs around 4 hours to set before assembling these slices, so do bear this in mind when making it.

MAKES 5 SLICES

1 quantity Puff pastry (see page 16)
plain (all-purpose) flour, for dusting

For the filling
2 sheets gelatine (I use Dr Oetker)
60g (2oz/5 tablespoons) caster (superfine) sugar
30g (1oz/scant ¼ cup) cornflour (cornstarch)
6 egg yolks
250ml (8½fl oz/1 cup plus 1 tablespoon) full-fat milk
250ml (8½fl oz/1 cup plus 1 tablespoon) double (heavy) cream
2 teaspoons vanilla bean paste

For the topping
100g (3½oz) ready-to-roll fondant icing
cornflour (cornstarch), for dusting
20g (¾oz/1½ tablespoons) unsalted butter, melted
25g (1oz) dark chocolate (optional)
edible flowers (optional)

ALTERNATIVE & CREATIVE PASTRY

● GF | IP | SW
○ CH | SH | VIE

Make the pastry following the recipe on page 16. After the final fold, rest in the fridge for 1 hour, or until needed.

Soak the gelatine sheets in cold water. Add the sugar, cornflour (cornstarch) and egg yolks to a large bowl, whisking together to combine. Heat the milk, cream and vanilla in a large saucepan until just boiling. Pour a little of the hot cream onto the egg mix and combine before adding the rest. Stir well, then return the custard to the pan. Bring back to the boil and allow to bubble, pop and thicken for 2 minutes, stirring continuously. Remove from the heat.

Drain the softened gelatine and pat dry with kitchen paper before adding it to the hot custard. Mix well to dissolve, then transfer to a clean bowl, allowing it to cool before whizzing in a food processor until silky. Transfer to a piping bag fitted with a plain 1cm (½in) nozzle and place in the fridge for at least 4 hours, or until needed.

As the filling sets, bake the pastry. If the pastry has been made in advance and has been in the fridge for longer than 1 hour, see page 19 before rolling it out. Lightly dust the pastry with flour and roll out to 5mm (¼in) depth, trying your best to keep it in a rectangular shape. Score a rectangle measuring 25 x 20cm (10 x 8in) onto the pastry rectangle, a little in from the edge all round, then within that score 10 smaller rectangles measuring 5 x 10cm (2 x 4in). The idea is to indent the pastry, not cut it. The best tool for this job, I have found, is a

pizza wheel – just press lightly. When all rolled, scored and ready, place the pastry on a baking tray lined with non-stick baking paper and pop in the fridge for 30 minutes.

Preheat the oven to 180°C (350°F), Gas Mark 4. Top the pastry with another sheet of non-stick baking paper and onto that lay another baking tray. Place in the oven and bake under the weight for 30 minutes, after which time carefully remove the top tray and bake for a further 10 minutes. The pastry should be crisp and deep golden. Remove from the oven and transfer to a wire rack, allowing to cool fully before slicing and assembling.

Roll out the fondant to a 1mm thickness (or as thinly as possible) – doing this between sheets of baking paper with a dusting of cornflour (cornstarch) will prevent sticking. Cut into five rectangles, each measuring 5 x 10cm (2 x 4in), and keep underneath the paper to prevent it drying.

Use a serrated knife to cut the baked pastry, using the pre-marked measurements as a guide. Lightly brush the tops of five rectangles with melted butter and place the rolled and cut fondant on top – using the butter to glue the icing in place. Pipe the custard onto the remaining five pastry rectangles and top with the iced pieces. Melt the chocolate in a bowl set over a pan of simmering water and use to decorate. The addition of an edible Phlox flower makes these custard slices extra pretty.

TARTIFLETTE PIES

Double carbs, it's a great phrase, and whenever I hear it I immediately want to eat whatever it is being used to describe! These little pies certainly deliver on the comfort front – creamy on the inside, golden on the outside, the hot water pastry providing a gratifying crunch. This recipe can be successfully made into one larger pie if you prefer.

MAKES 8 SMALL OVAL PIES,
using specialist tins measuring 5.5 x 10 x
4cm (2¼ x 4in x 1½in), see suppliers on
page 202

1 quantity of Hot Water pastry (see page 14)
plain (all-purpose) flour, for dusting
egg wash (see page 38)

For the filling
500g (18oz) waxy salad potatoes, sliced to
   8mm (⅜in) thick
fine salt, for the cooking water
1 tablespoon olive oil
200g (7oz) smoked pancetta lardons
20g (scant ¾oz/1 tablespoon) unsalted
   butter
200g (7oz) sweet red onions, finely
   sliced
1 large garlic clove, finely sliced
1 tablespoon thyme leaves
Maldon salt and black pepper
2 tablespoons plain (all-purpose) flour
200ml (6¾fl oz/¾ cup plus 2 tablespoons)
   double (heavy) cream
100ml (3⅓fl oz/⅓ cup plus 1 tablespoon)
   milk
40g (1½oz) Reblochon cheese, rind removed

ALTERNATIVE & CREATIVE PASTRY

● S
○ GF | SH | VIE

Make the pastry following the recipe on page 14, continuing up to and including the fridge resting. It may be beneficial to grease and flour your pie moulds, even if they are non-stick – just in case.

Cook the sliced potatoes in a pan of well-seasoned boiling water for 4 minutes. Drain and keep to one side. Heat a large frying pan, add the olive oil and pancetta and fry until the fat has softened and the meat is golden. Remove from the pan using a slotted spoon and drain on kitchen paper. Into the same pan, add the butter along with the onions, garlic, thyme, a sprinkling of salt and a grinding of black pepper. Slowly fry over a gentle heat until soft and golden, stirring occasionally. Add the flour and cook for another minute, stirring. Finally, add the cream and milk and simmer for 2 minutes to make a thick sauce.

Add the potatoes and pancetta, mix well, check the seasoning and adjust if needed. Allow the mixture to cool completely. Roll the pastry onto a lightly floured work surface to approximately 3mm (⅛in) depth. Cut 16 pieces from the pastry – eight for the bases and eight for the lids (shape depending on the tins being used) – then cut eight strips for the pie walls. Again, the measurements depend on the tins being used. Return to the fridge for at least 30 minutes.

Remove the pastry from the fridge and lay one oval into the base of each tin, pushing the pastry tightly into the sides. Brush the outer edges with egg wash and then use one cut strip per pie to make the pie wall, adhering the sides

to the base, pushing down well to seal. Now push the pastry into the sides of the tin and secure the ends of each strip by overlapping each, using egg wash as a glue. As an extra leakproof precaution, I like to roll a thin strip of pastry to use to push into all the seams. Simply adhere the thinly rolled pastry filler with more egg wash and push into place well using a floured finger. Repeat for the remaining ovals. Place back in the fridge, along with the remaining 8 ovals (lids), for at least 30 minutes. Reserve the remaining egg wash for later.

Half-fill the pie shells with the potato mixture, then add small pieces of cheese (surprisingly, 5g (¼oz) is enough for each pie), top with more potato, filling almost but not quite to the top of each tin. Brush the very tops of the pie sides with egg wash and secure a pastry lid to each, pressing down well to seal. Add some extra pastry garnishes if you want to, securing each addition in place with egg wash. When done, brush each pie top evenly with egg wash and add an inconspicuous steam hole using a skewer or similar. Put the pies in the fridge for at least 1 hour.

Preheat the oven to 180°C (350°F), Gas Mark 4. Bake the pies in the oven (if using individual tins, place onto a baking sheet) for 40 minutes before carefully removing the pies from their tins. Egg wash the sides then return to the oven for a further 5 minutes, until beautifully golden and crisp. When fully baked, remove from the oven and rest upon a wire rack until just warm – the optimum temperature at which to enjoy these pies.

NANA MAUD'S CUSTARD TART

My mother was a great cook, and so too was her mother, and because of their love of cooking and feeding, many of my fondest childhood memories are food-related. Their food was simple, rustic and frugal, but it was always delicious and served with love. There were a few stand-out dishes – those that I can almost taste when thinking of them – including the best roast beef dinner, a juicy black pudding and lamb tatty pot, condensed milk on toast (don't ask), and this... Nana Maud's epic custard tart.

SERVES 8–10,
using a loose-bottomed 18 x 4cm (7 x
**   1½in) circular tin**

1 quantity Sweet Shortcrust pastry (see page 12)

For the filling
170g (6oz) egg yolks
85g (3oz/7 tablespoons) granulated sugar
500ml (17fl oz/2 cups plus 2 tablespoons) double (heavy) cream
fresh nutmeg, for grating

Make the pastry following the recipe on page 12. After resting it in the fridge, line, blind bake and trim a pastry case, using the tips and techniques on page 38. Leave the baked case inside the tin.

Preheat the oven to 120°C (250°F), Gas Mark ½ – I strongly recommend using an oven thermometer for this, unless you really know your oven.

Place the egg yolks in a large bowl, and add the sugar to a pan with the cream over a low heat. Allow the sugar to dissolve, then heat very gently until it reaches 37°C/99°F (or as my Nana used to say, 'hand warm'). Pour this over the egg yolks, mix to combine – trying your best not to incorporate too much air – then strain through a sieve into a jug or something that can be easily poured from.

Position a baking tray in the oven, fairly low down, and remove all the racks above. Place the pastry case onto the baking tray, then pour the custard into the tart shell, filling as close to the top as possible. Grate a blanket of nutmeg over the surface and bake for 40 minutes before checking the wobble. My trick is to very gently bang on the closed oven door, looking at the wobble through the glass. A slight ripple towards the centre is what's needed. If the ripple extends further, bake for up to 15 minutes more, but check the wobble after each additional 5 minutes.

I guess knowing the perfect wobble comes from practice – practice and knowledge that the tart will set further upon cooling.

Remove from the oven and allow to cool completely at room temperature before removing from the tin. Slice into generous portions to serve.

No accompaniments are needed here, it is quite simply perfection as is.

FROMAGE BLANC, HONEYCOMB AND FIG VIENNOISERIE

I love how viennoiserie is so popular again, with specialist bakeries and cafés opening up across the country, selling nothing but these delicious snacks. These artisan hot spots often have queues of customers lining the pavements outside, eagerly awaiting some freshly baked pastries to enjoy with exceptional coffee.

It is possible to make great viennoiserie at home with a bit of practice and plenty of patience – be warned, it's not a speedy process. If you want to enjoy these pastries with a morning coffee, follow the timeline on page 28 and allow them to prove overnight in the fridge, ready to be baked fresh the following morning.

MAKES 6

1 quantity Viennoiserie pastry (see page 26)
plain (all-purpose) flour, for dusting
egg wash (see page 38)

For the filling
120g (4¼oz) fromage blanc
2 tablespoons caster (superfine) sugar
1 teaspoon vanilla bean paste
6 teaspoons fig jam (shop-bought is fine)
3 fresh figs, halved
3 tablespoons runny honey

To finish (all optional)
60g (2¼oz) natural honeycomb
icing (powdered) sugar
edible flowers

ALTERNATIVE & CREATIVE PASTRY

● IP | P
○ CH | GF | SH | SW

Make the dough up to and including the final fridge resting, following the recipe and guidance on page 26.

When fully rested, roll the dough onto a lightly floured work surface to an approximate thickness of 5mm (¼in), however, please refer to the notes on page 28 before doing so, if helpful. Cut into six squares, each measuring 10 x 10cm (4 x 4in). Lay each piece of pastry onto a large baking sheet lined with non-stick baking paper. Fold the four corners into the centre of each, pushing down well to secure in place. To prevent the middle of the pastry from rising during proving and baking, make a weight for each. Line an egg cup with three layers of ovenproof cling film, then fill it with baking beans. Twist the top of the cling film, securing the beans in place, to make a ball. Place this ball on to the centre of the folded pastry. Repeat for all. Loosely cover with cling film and allow to prove in a warm place for up to 3 hours (for more guidance on timings and proving, see page 28).

Preheat the oven to 180°C (350°F), Gas Mark 4. Brush the smooth surfaces of each pastry with egg wash, being careful not to let any drip into the layers. Bake in the oven for 20–25 minutes, or until dark golden. Don't be tempted to take the pastries out of the oven too early; the longer bake will ensure the crunch and delicious flakiness that is so desirable. When done, remove the weight from each and allow to cool on wire racks.

When the pastries are cool, mix together the fromage blanc mixture, sugar and vanilla for the filling. Place a teaspoon of the fig jam into the centre of each pastry basket, top each with a tablespoon of the fromage blanc, then top with a fig half. Gently warm the runny honey in a pan, then brush the cut surface of the figs with it. Add a nugget of honeycomb to each, if using, dust over some icing (powdered) sugar and add a flower or two if you fancy. (Remember that edible flowers should be chosen for flavour and not only for decor; here I have used Mallow and Phlox flowers as they are both subtle and delicate in flavour.)

Eat on the day of making.

GOAT'S CHEESE AND FENNEL JAM GALETTE

Recipe development is quite a process. Sometimes recipes are worked out during hands-on cooking and tasting, sometimes I simply imagine how ingredients will work together. Some work, some don't, some evolve and make the grade, some will never be made again. When I first imagined a fennel jam, I knew it would be good, but I wasn't expecting it to be this good. My imagination had done me proud. This fennel jam proves to be the perfect accompaniment to goat's cheese.

The quantities given for the jam will make double of what is needed for this recipe, but that's a good thing, as I do believe you'll want to make this galette again pretty soon.

SERVES 4–6

1 quantity Salted Shortcrust pastry (see page 10)
plain (all purpose) flour, for dusting
egg wash (see page 38)

For the fennel jam

500g (18oz) or 2 large fennel bulbs, fronds trimmed and reserved, roots removed
250ml (8½fl oz/1 cup plus 1 tablespoon) water
200g (7oz/1 cup) jam sugar
juice of ½ lemon
1 teaspoon Maldon salt
black pepper
½ teaspoon very finely chopped garlic
¼ teaspoon toasted fennel seeds
1 tablespoon finely chopped parsley

For the topping

200g (7oz) Golden Cross (rinded) goat's cheese log, or suitable alternative
½ teaspoon fennel seeds
100g (3½oz) Innes goat's curd, or other variety (optional)

ALTERNATIVE & CREATIVE PASTRY

● GF | HW
○ SH | VIE

Make the pastry following the instructions on page 10. Roll out between cling film to 3mm (⅛in), trying your best to keep it in a circular shape. Rest at room temperature between the cling film until needed.

Halve each fennel bulb, then finely slice across each half. Place in a saucepan with the water, jam sugar and lemon juice and bring to a simmer, allowing to gently bubble for 40 minutes, stirring occasionally. After this time, the sugary water will have reduced to a sticky glaze that coats the fennel slices. Chop the reserved fronds and add to the jam along with the remaining seasonings. Allow to cool completely.

Remove the cling film from the pastry and transfer to a sheet of non-stick baking paper. Trim to neaten, or if preferred, leave as is for a more rustic finish, as pictured.

Spread half of the cooled jam over the pastry, covering all but a 3cm (1¼in) border. Slice the rinded goat's cheese log into 1cm (½in) thick rounds and place on top of the fennel jam. Sprinkle with salt, then fold up the uncovered pastry, creating an encasing border, then place in the fridge for at least 30 minutes.

Place a baking sheet into the oven and preheat the oven to 180°C (350°F), Gas Mark 4. Brush the pastry with the egg wash. Cover the cheese with kitchen foil and bake in the oven for 30 minutes. Remove the foil and bake for a further 15 minutes, by which time the pastry and the goat's cheese will be golden.

Remove from the oven, spoon dots of the soft goat's curd in and around the galette, sprinkle with the toasted fennel seeds and serve immediately.

Sweet cicely fronds, if used sparingly, work beautifully with this galette due to its aniseed flavour.

Chickweed

Mallow flower

Wild pea

Sweet cicley

Dill

Bronze fennel

Mange tout

Yarrow

SUPER SLOW ONION AND GRUYÈRE TART

The humble onion is such an indispensable ingredient, used in kitchens the world over. They are often the unsung hero of many a savoury dish, doing their job unassumingly and often unnoticed in the background.

This tart showcases onions; by slowly roasting and basting them in a buttery stock they become soft, caramelized and sweetened, yet still satisfyingly savoury. So simple, but so, so good.

SERVES 6–8,

using a 25 x 2cm (10 x ¾in) fluted, loose-bottomed circular tin

1 quantity Salted Shortcrust pastry (see page 10)
egg wash (see page 38)

For the onions
60g (2oz/¼ cup) unsalted butter, softened
¼ teaspoon nigella seeds (optional)
1 tablespoon thyme leaves
finely grated zest of ½ lemon
1 tablespoon runny honey
1 teaspoon Maldon salt
½ teaspoon cracked black pepper
6 small brown onions, cut in half horizontally, skin on
150ml (5fl oz/⅔ cup) dry white wine
150ml (5fl oz/⅔ cup) chicken or vegetable stock
olive oil, for drizzling

For the savoury custard
60g (2oz) Gruyère, finely grated
3 eggs
150ml (5fl oz/⅔ cup) milk
100ml (3½fl oz/⅓ cup) double (heavy) cream
1 tablespoon finely chopped chives
Maldon salt and black pepper

ALTERNATIVE & CREATIVE PASTRY

● HW
○ SH

Make the pastry following the recipe on page 10. After resting, use the pastry to line, blind bake and trim a tart case – see tips on page 38. Save any remaining pastry for another use.

Preheat the oven to 180°C (350°F), Gas Mark 4. For the onions, add to the softened butter the nigella (if using), the thyme, lemon zest, honey, salt and pepper. Lay the halved onions snugly in a small roasting tray, cut-side up. Smooth a generous layer of flavoured butter over the surface of each onion half, then pour the wine and stock into the side of the tray. Drizzle lightly with olive oil and roast, uncovered, in the oven for 1½ hours, basting with the buttery stock every 15 minutes or so. If after the first hour the onion tops are burning, finish the cooking time with a layer of kitchen foil covering the tray.

Remove from the oven and allow to cool in the tray, after which time, carefully remove the skins while trying to keep the onions intact in their halves. Reduce the oven temperature to 120°C (250°F), Gas Mark ½.

Place the grated cheese in the bottom of the prepared pastry case, then lay the onions in and around the bed of cheese. In a small bowl, mix together the eggs, milk and cream, then sprinkle in the chives. Add some salt and pepper, then pour the custard into the tart shell, leaving the tops of the onions exposed.

Place on a baking sheet and bake in the oven for 1 hour, or until the custard has almost set – look for a slight wobble towards the centre.

Allow to cool sufficiently on a wire rack before removing the tart from the tin. Serve either warm or cold with a seasonal green salad. Unusual leaves and savoury leaf flowers can make a dish shine and are worth sourcing; I absolutely love Yarrow leaves, the beautiful fronds that are pictured.

DOUBLE CHOC ÉCLAIRS WITH VANILLA CARAMEL

The humble éclair has made a rather snazzy comeback, thanks to Joakim Prat of Maître Choux. His embellished pastries are so pretty, and famously displayed – bright, uniform and inviting, the selection of flavour combinations are unusual and appealing. While I have kept the flavourings pretty classic here, I couldn't resist the inspired embellishments. The easiest way to achieve consistent size and shape is to use an éclair mould, which can easily be found online. However, this is not essential – piping free-form will also give great results.

MAKES 20,
using a 12 x 2.5cm (4½ x 1in) éclair mould

1 quantity Choux pastry (see page 24)

For the craquelin (optional)
50g (1¾oz/3½ tablespoons) unsalted butter, softened
50g (1¾oz/¼ cup) caster (superfine) sugar
50g (1¾oz/6 tablespoons) plain (all-purpose) flour

For chocolate cream filling
120g (4¼oz) dark chocolate
6 egg yolks
120g (4¼oz/⅔ cup minus 2 teaspoons) caster (superfine) sugar
40g (1½oz/3¼oz) plain (all-purpose) flour
20g (⅔oz/2 tablespoons plus 4 teaspoons) cornflour (cornstarch)
500ml (17fl oz/2 cups plus 2 tablespoons) milk

For the caramel
150g (5¼oz/¾ cup) caster (superfine) sugar
100ml (3½fl oz/⅓ cup plus 1 tablespoon) water
20g (¾oz/1½ tablespoons) unsalted butter, cut into 1cm (½in) cubes
150ml (5fl oz/⅔ cup) double (heavy) cream
2 teaspoons vanilla bean paste
½ teaspoon Maldon salt

Decorations (all optional)
tempered chocolate shapes (see suppliers on page 202)
sprinkles
chocolate shavings
edible gold dust
edible flowers

ALTERNATIVE & CREATIVE PASTRY

○ GF | IP | P | SH | SW | VIE

Make the pastry following the recipe on page 24 and spoon into a piping bag fitted with a 1.5cm (⅝in) star-shaped nozzle, trying not to incorporate too much air. Leave to cool while making the topping and fillings.

If using a craquelin, mix all of the ingredients together to form a paste, then roll out between two sheets of non-stick baking paper to 1mm (or as thinly as possible) and place in the freezer for at least 30 minutes.

To make the cream filling, break the chocolate into small pieces and place them in a heatproof bowl set above a pan of simmering water, making sure the bowl is not touching the water. When the chocolate has melted, remove from the heat and set aside. Place the egg yolks and one-third of the sugar into a large bowl, whisk well then add the flours. Add the milk and the remaining sugar to a large saucepan and bring to the boil, removing from the heat as soon as it does. Pour the hot milk over the egg yolk mix in 3 stages, whisking continuously. Return to the pan and bring to a boil, then immediately reduce to a simmer and allow to bubble and thicken for a few minutes, whisking throughout. Transfer to a clean bowl, add the melted chocolate and stir until fully incorporated. Allow to cool completely, then blitz in a food processor until silky and smooth. Transfer to a piping bag fitted with a decorative nozzle.

To make the caramel, place the sugar and water in a frying pan and set over a medium heat. When the sugar has dissolved, keep a close eye on the liquid, but do not stir. As the sugar starts to caramelize and turn amber, swirl the pan around so that it colours evenly. When light-amber bubbles start to pop, add the butter, a little at a time, whisking between each addition. Add the cream, vanilla and salt, give one final whisk, then allow to bubble for a few minutes until thickened. Pass through a sieve into a bowl and allow to cool before transferring to a piping bag fitted with a small plain nozzle.

Preheat the oven to 180ºC (350ºF), Gas Mark 4. Pipe the choux into éclair moulds or onto a lined baking sheet (do this in batches if needs be), leaving a sufficient gap between each to allow for expansion during baking. Remove the craquelin (if using) from the freezer and cut 20 rectangles from it, the same width and length of the éclairs. Lay one rectangle of craquelin on top of each piped choux.

Bake in the oven for 20 minutes, then reduce the heat to 140ºC (275ºF), Gas Mark 1 and bake for a further 20 minutes. It is really important that the oven door remains closed during baking. After the 40 minutes, remove from the oven and pierce the bottom of each with a skewer, to allow the steam to escape. Transfer to a wire rack to cool.

Slice the éclairs in half horizontally, then pipe a small amount of the caramel onto each base. Top with a generous amount of the chocolate crème. Place the tops then use some of the caramel to stick the tempered chocolate on top, adding extra decorative flourishes, if you fancy. Eat fresh.

PASTIERA NAPOLETANA

I have a love affair with Italy, especially the Amalfi Coast. The dream is to one day retire there, write recipes, cook and bake – live the simple life. I was first introduced to Pastiera by my dear friend Maria, from Maiori, a town close to Amalfi. When visiting her the week before Easter, she was gathering all of the ingredients to make this festive bake: cedro (candied citron), pearl barley and orange blossom water. I was completely intrigued and naturally had to give it a try. It is wonderful and very different to anything I have ever baked before – and the aroma given off during baking is enchanting.

If, like me, you live somewhere that has limited specialist ingredients, or if cedro is in short supply, citrus zest makes a suitable and pleasing replacement.

SERVES 8–10,
using a deep, loose-bottomed 18 x 4cm
   (7 x 1½in) circular tin

1 quantity Sweet Shortcrust pastry (see
   page 12)
egg wash (see page 38)

For the pearl barley
100g (3½oz) pearl barley
500ml (17fl oz/2 cups plus 2 tablespoons)
   water
1 tablespoon caster (superfine) sugar
200ml (6¾fl oz/¾ cup plus 2 tablespoons)
   milk
30g (1oz/2 tablespoons) unsalted butter

For the filling
250g (8¾oz) soft ricotta cheese
200g (7oz) caster (superfine) sugar, plus
   extra for dusting
1 teaspoon vanilla extract
½ teaspoon ground cinnamon
1 tablespoon orange blossom water
1 tablespoon orange blossom honey
   (optional)
zest of 2 clementines
zest of ½ lemon
3 eggs, using 2 whole eggs and 1 yolk

To finish
icing (powdered) sugar

Make and rest the pastry following the recipe on page 12, then use to line, blind bake and trim a pastry case (see tips and techniques on page 38). Leave the case in the tin and save any excess pastry for later.

There's no need to soak the pearl barley, simply bring it to a simmer in a pan with the water and caster (superfine) sugar. Gently cook until all of the water has been absorbed, then add the milk and butter and continue to simmer, stirring continuously, until the milk has been absorbed and the barley looks like cooked porridge. Transfer to a bowl and allow to cool completely.

For the filling, whip the ricotta until smooth, then add all of the other filling ingredients. Do check the orange blossom water for concentration before adding – if it is double strength, adjust the amount according to the bottle instructions. Fold it all into the cooled grains and give it a thorough mix, without incorporating too much air.

Traditionally, the ricotta mixture is rested in the fridge for 24 hours, allowing the flavours to develop, which if you have the time you may wish to do, too. Either way, when ready, fill the tart shell so that it is almost full. There may be some mixture left over.

Preheat the oven to 160°C (325°F), Gas Mark 3. Roll out the reserved pastry and cut it into strips to lay across the top of the filling (a pasta machine fitted with a tagliatelle attachment is useful here, see page 36). A diamond-shaped criss-cross is traditional, yet extra or alternative décor could be added to suit personal style. Brush the pastry décor with egg wash and sprinkle with caster (superfine) sugar.

Place in the oven on a baking sheet and bake for 15 minutes, after which cover loosely with kitchen foil and continue to bake for 30 minutes more. Remove the foil and bake until the ricotta mixture has turned completely golden and the pastry décor is crisp – this should take another 30 minutes or so.

Remove from the oven and allow to cool in the tin. This pie is best eaten cold and is considered even better after an overnight rest in the fridge. However, do bring it back to room temperature to enjoy it at its best.

Dust with icing (powdered) sugar and serve with strong coffee.

CHAPTER 4

Nuts

PINE NUT PRALINE, RUM AND RAISIN PINWHEELS

I love rum and raisin ice cream, yet I couldn't really envelop that in pastry and bake it, although I did toy with the idea for a while. Instead, I played around with the flavour combinations, eventually coming up with these pastries, which most definitely hit the spot. Creamy, boozy, fruity and utterly delicious, these would be excellent served with coffee or, better still, a rum-spiked coffee!

MAKES 6

1 quantity Viennoiserie pastry (see page 26)
plain (all-purpose) flour, for dusting
egg wash (see page 38)

For the praline

150g (5⅓oz/¾ cup) caster (superfine) sugar
pinch of salt
150ml (5fl oz/⅔ cup) water
100g (3½oz) pine nuts, toasted

For the crème pâtissière

2 egg yolks
40g (1½oz/3 tablespoons) caster (superfine) sugar
15g (½oz/1¾ tablespoons) plain (all-purpose) flour
10g (¼oz/1 tablespoon) cornflour (cornstarch)
160ml (5fl oz/⅔ cup plus 1 tablespoon) milk
½ teaspoon vanilla bean paste (optional)

For the raisins

30g (1oz) golden raisins
50ml (2fl oz/3½ tablespoons) dark rum

To finish

reserved pine nut praline
4 tablespoons icing (powdered) sugar mixed with a few drops of water

ALTERNATIVE & CREATIVE PASTRY

● IP | P
○ CH | GF | SH | SW

Make the pastry following the recipe on page 26. During the proving and folding process, make and prepare the fillings and toppings.

To make the praline, place the sugar, salt and water in a frying pan and set over a medium heat. When the sugar has dissolved, keep a close eye on the liquid, but do not stir. As the sugar starts to caramelize and turn amber, swirl the contents of the pan around so that it colours evenly. Tip the toasted pine nuts into the caramel and very briefly stir to combine. Immediately pour onto a non-stick baking mat or non-stick baking paper. Allow to cool.

For the crème pâtissière, follow the method on page 48, adding the cornflour at the same time as the plain flour.

When both praline and crème pâtissière have cooled completely, break the praline into small pieces. Place all but a quarter of the praline in a food processor along with the crème pâtissière and blitz until completely smooth. Transfer to a piping bag and chill in the fridge. Store the remaining praline in an airtight container.

To soak the raisins, heat both the raisins and rum in a small pan and allow to gently simmer for 1 minute, then turn off the heat and allow the fruit to sit in the alcohol. If soaked for long enough the raisins will completely absorb the rum.

When the dough is ready, roll out using the techniques as described on page 28. Cut into six squares, each measuring

9 x 9cm (3½ x 3½in), then make a 3cm (1¼in) incision from each corner point in towards the centre of each square. Fold alternate points in towards the centre, securing each by pressing down firmly. Transfer to a baking sheet lined with non-stick baking paper, allowing enough room between each for expansion.

Blind bake these pastries. To do this you need a weight for each (placed in the centre) – a small handful of baking beans wrapped in ovenproof cling film works perfectly if layered by three. Cover each pastry loosely with cling film and allow to prove for up to 3 hours (please see proving notes on page 28). Be careful not to leave them in too warm a place, as the butter may melt.

Preheat the oven to 180°C (350°F), Gas Mark 4. Brush the pastry tops with egg wash, brushing only the smooth surfaces and not the layers. Bake in the oven for 35 minutes, or until the pastry is deep golden, crisp and flaking. Remove the weight from each, then allow to cool on a wire rack. When cold, pop a few raisins into the cavity of each pastry, top with the pine nut crème, add a few more raisins and finish with some of the reserved pine nut praline and a drizzle of water icing.

TREACLE TART DELUXE

This is a classic British tart, made traditionally using cheap ingredients. Comforting, sticky, sweet and nostalgic, it is a dessert that I was fed as a child, and which, therefore, I love. I have added some cream and almonds to my recipe, which although makes it more calorific, I'd say is definitely worth it. You may find a small portion of this tart to be enough, due to its sweetness. My preferred accompaniment for this is a thick Greek-style yoghurt – coconut-flavoured, preferably. Not quite the canned evaporated milk that my Nana would have poured over hers!

Some consider this tart to be even better the next day, after an overnight chilling in the fridge.

SERVES 10–12,
using a loose-bottomed 20 x 3.5cm (8 x
**   1½in) circular tin**

1 quantity Sweet Shortcrust pastry (see
   page 12)

For the filling
75g (2¾oz) fresh white breadcrumbs
340g (12oz) golden syrup
75g (2¾oz) ground almonds
150ml (5fl oz/⅔ cup) double (heavy) cream
2 eggs, lightly beaten
flaked almonds (optional)
Maldon salt flakes, for sprinkling

ALTERNATIVE & CREATIVE PASTRY

● GF

Make the pastry following the recipe on page 12. After resting, line the tin with the pastry, blind bake and then trim, using the tips and method on page 38. Leave the cooked pastry case in the tin.

Preheat the oven to 150°C (300°F), Gas Mark 2. Tip the breadcrumbs into a dry frying pan set over a medium heat. Allow the crumbs to toast and turn golden in the pan, stirring or shaking every so often to prevent them burning. When beautifully golden, transfer to a plate.

Gently heat the syrup in a saucepan over a low heat, then add the breadcrumbs and ground almonds, mixing well. Remove from the heat and add the cream and eggs, combine well without incorporating too much air.

Place the prepared pastry case onto a baking sheet and fill the case to the top with the syrup mixture. Decoratively

lay some flaked almonds over the top, if using, and sprinkle over a few salt flakes. Transfer to the oven and bake for 40 minutes, but check after 35 minutes, unless you know your oven well. The tart is ready when the top has developed a crust yet is still slightly wobbling towards the centre.

When done, remove from the oven and allow to cool fully, after which remove from the tin, slice and serve alongside coconut yogurt.

WALNUT, PEAR AND REGALIS TARTE FINES

The combination of soft fruit, tangy cheese and toasted nuts is undeniably heaven, and the nuts and seeds within the gluten-free pastry make the perfect platform on which to serve this, making a very tasty and sophisticated lunch, starter or light supper. Admittedly, Regalis cheese isn't easy to find, but if you can source some, I promise it will be worth it – sweet yet sharp, salty and slightly floral, it is truly unforgettable. If you are ever in London, make sure to pop into a branch of La Fromagerie to grab some. If you can't find Regalis, Roquefort would work well.

MAKES 6 TARTS

1 quantity Salted Gluten-free pastry (see page 32)
cornflour (cornstarch), for dusting

For the pear
100ml (3⅓fl oz/⅓ cup plus 1 tablespoon) pear cordial, diluted with 100ml water, or 200ml (7fl oz) water
50g (1¾oz/¼ cup) caster (superfine) sugar
juice of 1 lemon
1 firm pear, washed

For the topping
150g (5½oz) Regalis, crumbled into small pieces
80g (2¾oz) walnuts, toasted and crushed
1 punnet blackberries, halved
interesting salad leaves, such as tagete, pea shoots and purple radish

To finish
extra virgin olive oil, for drizzling
runny honey, for drizzling
Maldon salt and black pepper
rocket flowers, if in season (optional)

ALTERNATIVE & CREATIVE PASTRY

● HW | IP | S
○ CH | P | SH | VIE

Make the pastry following the recipe on page 32. Roll between two sheets of non-stick baking paper to around 5mm (¼in) thick; if it's sticking, dust with cornflour (cornstarch). Leave to rest in the fridge for at least 30 minutes.

Preheat the oven to 180°C (350°F), Gas Mark 4. Line a baking sheet with non-stick baking paper. Cut the pastry into six squares, each measuring approximately 10 x 10cm (4 x 4in). Place on the lined baking sheet. Prick the surface of each square with a fork, then score a border 1cm (½in) on each. There's no need to egg wash the pastry, simply bake in the oven for 15–20 minutes, until golden and crisp. Remove from the oven and allow to cool on a wire rack.

As the pear will brown quickly, gather all of the other ingredients first and have them ready for assembling. Mix together the cordial, water, sugar and lemon juice in a pan, then gently heat until just starting to simmer. Finely slice the pear vertically, either by hand or use a mandolin, then submerge the slices in the simmering liquid for 2–3 minutes, until pliable but not breaking. Drain and set to one side.

Divide all of the topping ingredients evenly among the baked pastry squares, and fold and nestle a pear slice between the leaves. Drizzle with olive oil and honey then finish with a flourish of salt and pepper and some rocket flowers, if you like. Serve immediately.

FRANGIPANE, PERSIMMON AND GRAPE TART

Persimmons have gained in popularity in the UK over recent years. They regularly feature in the fruit aisles in our supermarkets, where once they could never be found. With a sweet honey flavour, high nutritional value and health benefits aplenty, it is easy to see why they have become the fastest-selling exotic fruit in the UK in recent years.

The vibrant edible skin of the fruit lends itself well to this bake, creating an eye-catching Insta-grammable tart, both pre and post bake.

SERVES 8–10,
using a deep, circular, loose-bottomed tart tin measuring 21 x 3.5cm (8¼ x 1½in)

1 quantity Sweet Shortcrust pastry (see page 12)
egg wash (see page 38)

For the persimmon butter
6 ripe persimmons, topped, peeled and cut into 1cm (½in) cubes
100g (3½oz/½ cup) caster (superfine) sugar
1 teaspoon vanilla bean paste
juice of 2 clementines
40g (1½oz/3 tablespoons) unsalted butter

For the frangipane
75g (2¾oz/⅓ cup) unsalted butter, at room temperature
75g (2¾oz/6 tablespoons) caster (superfine) sugar
75g (2¾oz) ground almonds
75g (2¾oz) eggs (shelled weight), lightly beaten

To decorate
6 persimmons, firm not overly ripe
large handful of black seedless grapes, halved
cut-out pastry decorations

To finish
caster (superfine) sugar, for sprinkling
cream, to serve (optional)

ALTERNATIVE & CREATIVE PASTRY

● GF

Make the pastry following the recipe on page 12. After resting, line the tin with the pastry, blind bake and then trim, using the tips and method on page 38. Leave the baked pastry case in the tin for later. Any spare pastry can be cut into shapes and used to make decorations later.

To make the persimmon butter, place the chopped fruit in a pan with the sugar and vanilla and cook gently for 5 minutes. Add the clementine juice and continue to simmer for 30–40 minutes, stirring occasionally until thickened. When thick, add the butter, stir well, then remove from the heat and allow to cool in a bowl. Blitz to a smooth paste with a food blender, then set to one side.

To make the frangipane, place the soft butter into the bowl of a freestanding mixer (or mix by hand), along with the caster (superfine) sugar. Attach the paddle and beat for 1 minute. Add the ground almonds and eggs alternately in three consecutive bursts, beating continuously between additions. Combine well.

Add a layer of persimmon butter to the tart case, spreading it out evenly. Top that with a generous layer of frangipane, until the case is two-thirds full. Store any remaining persimmon butter and frangipane in the fridge for another use. The persimmon butter will last for a week in the fridge, and the frangipane will last for 5 days.

Preheat the oven to 160°C (325°F), Gas Mark 3. To decorate the tart, prepare the remaining persimmons by removing the leaves and cutting the fruits in half vertically. Using either a mandolin or a sharp knife, slice each half across the width to 1mm (or as thinly as possible). Also have the grape halves and any cut pastry shapes to hand. Arrange the fruit in the frangipane in a decorative manner using any pastry shapes for added decoration. If pastry décor is used, brush each piece with egg wash prior to baking. Sprinkle a fine layer of caster (superfine) sugar over the entire surface, cover with kitchen foil and bake in the oven for up to 2 hours. I find baking for a longer spell, underneath foil, helps to intensify the fruit flavour and prevents any excessive colouring to the edges. Do check the tart occasionally and remove the foil towards the end of baking, to allow the pastry to colour.

Allow to cool for at least 10 minutes in the tin before removing and slicing. Serve warm or cold – with cream, if you like.

PARIS BREST WITH CHERRIES AND DIPPED HAZELNUTS

Paris Brest is a traditional French classic that can be easily found in many patisseries the world over. It's a bit of a showstopper, especially with the addition of the dipped hazelnuts, and could make a fun alternative to a birthday cake. I have added cherries here as they were in season, however other fruits work well, too – raspberries, blackberries and even blackcurrants. This is equally as delicious as is, so leave out the fruit if preferred.

SERVES 6–8

1 quantity Choux pastry (see page 24)
egg wash (see page 38)
flaked almonds, for sprinkling

For the praline paste
150g (5⅓oz/¾ cup) caster (superfine) sugar
pinch of salt
50ml (1⅔fl oz/3½ tablespoons) water
80g (2¾oz) blanched almonds, toasted
80g (2¾oz) blanched hazelnuts, toasted

For the crème pâtissière
3 egg yolks
40g (1½oz/3¼ tablespoons) caster (superfine) sugar
20g (¾oz/2⅓ tablespoons) plain (all-purpose) flour
10g (⅓oz/1 tablespoon plus 2 teaspoons) cornflour (cornstarch)
250ml (8½fl oz/1 cup plus 1 tablespoon) milk
1 teaspoon vanilla bean paste

To finish
fresh cherries, halved, stones removed (optional)
icing (powdered) sugar
dipped caramel hazelnuts (optional – see note overleaf)

ALTERNATIVE & CREATIVE PASTRY

○ GF | IP | P | SH | SW | VE

Make the pastry following the recipe on page 24. Spoon into a piping bag fitted with a 1cm (½in) star-shaped nozzle, trying not to incorporate too much air. The choux can be piped onto non-stick baking paper freehand or, if easier, draw around two plates onto the paper to create a template. First draw around a plate measuring approximately 20cm (8in) in diameter, then place a smaller plate, approximately 10cm (4in) in diameter into the centre of that and draw around it. Turn the paper over (otherwise the pen will transfer to the baked choux) and secure the baking paper to a baking sheet using a little of the choux paste. Pipe the choux, using the template to guide you – I tend to pipe inside the outer circle first, then around the inner circle, then I fill the middle lastly, creating a complete ring.

Preheat the oven to 180°C (350°F), Gas Mark 4. Brush the piped choux with egg wash, then sprinkle some flaked almonds on top. Bake in the oven for 40 minutes. It is important not to open the door during baking, as the choux needs to expand and set. After 40 minutes, turn the oven down to 140°C (275°F), Gas Mark 1, and bake for a further 20 minutes, after which time remove from the oven and pierce around the bottom of the ring with a skewer to allow any steam to escape. Allow to cool completely on a wire rack.

To make the praline paste, heat the sugar, salt and water in a pan until the sugar caramelizes – do not stir it,

occasionally swirl the pan instead so the sugar colours evenly. Once it is deep golden, take the pan off the heat, tip in the toasted nuts and stir to combine, immediately pour onto a non-stick baking mat or sheet of non-stick baking paper and allow to cool completely.

Meanwhile, make the crème pâtissière. Add the egg yolks and one-third of the sugar to a large bowl and whisk until the yolks are pale and have some volume. Add the flours and whisk to combine. In a large saucepan, bring the milk, the remaining sugar and the vanilla to the boil, then remove from the heat immediately. Pour a little of the hot milk over the egg yolks, whisking continuously, then add the remainder. Pour the custard back into the pan and bring to a gentle boil, whisking. Allow the custard to bubble and thicken for about 2 minutes, whisking throughout. Once thickened, remove from the pan and place in a bowl, covering the surface with a layer of cling film before it cools, to prevent a skin forming.

When the praline has fully set and cooled, break it into small pieces and place in a food processor. Add the cooled crème and blend together until smooth. The timing for this will depend on the power of the processor being used. When smooth, transfer to a piping bag fitted with a star-shaped nozzle and place in the fridge for at least 1 hour.

Continued overleaf

Carefully slice the baked choux in half horizontally, removing the top half. Fill the base of the ring with the nutty crème and place the halved cherries around the outer edge, if using. Replace the choux lid and dust with icing (powdered) sugar. If wanting to use dipped hazelnuts to decorate, see the note to the right and place on top of your Paris Brest.

*If you are making the pulled dipped hazelnuts, use blanched, skinned hazelnuts and gather one cocktail stick per hazelnut being dipped. It is always a good idea to dip more than is required so you can pick the best ones. Pierce the base of each hazelnut with the tip of a cocktail stick, just enough so that it stays in place, yet not too far in that the nut splits. Repeat with all of the nuts and set to one side. Have a large bowl of iced water and a pastry brush dipped in water to hand, then select a saucepan that will fit into the bowl. Secure a thick strip of sticky tack to the underside of a kitchen cupboard and directly under that lay a baking tray in which to catch the caramel drips... it will all make sense soon!

In the saucepan, dissolve 200g (7oz) of caster (superfine) sugar with 100ml (3½fl oz) of water and set over a medium heat. Allow to bubble until the liquid changes colour, first from light through to dark amber. It is important not to stir the caramel as it colours, simply swirl the pan so that the caramelization is even. Use the dipped pastry brush to run around the insides of the pan a few times during the process, to prevent crystallization. When the caramel is dark amber, dip the base of the pan into the iced water, stopping the caramel from darkening further. Allow to sit in the water for a minute or two until the caramel starts to stiffen. The best way to tell when it is ready is to keep dipping and lifting a skewered hazelnut from the caramel. If the caramel is coating the nut well, it is time to start.

Rest the pan of caramel so that it is close to the sticky tack'd cupboard. Carefully dip a skewered hazelnut into the caramel, turn it a little, then lift it out slowly. Attach the other end of the cocktail stick firmly into the sticky tack so that the nut is hanging upside down. The excess caramel will drip from the nut, setting hard as it cools, creating what will be a beautiful caramel spike when turned upright. Repeat until all of the hazelnuts have been dipped and dripped.

If when working the caramel siezes, gently warm it through over a low heat until it returns to the correct consistency.

PEANUT AND POTATO SATAY BITES

Granted, this recipe is unusual, and the inspirations reach far and wide. It shows that working with pastry has endless possibilities to explore, a versatile component that allows for experimentation. The layering here was inspired by baklava, the sweet and sticky pistachio treat of Turkey and the Middle East. Here I've replaced the honeyed nuts with curried peanuts, the sweet syrup changed to a sticky chilli sauce. These tasty bites make a perfect appetizer and also work as a starter, just offset the sweetness of a larger portion with something sharp.

SERVES 6–12,
using a loose-bottomed 20 x 4cm (8 x 1½in) square tin

1 quantity Sheet pastry (see page 30)
cornflour (cornstarch), for dusting
coconut oil, melted, for brushing

For the filling
140g (5oz) potato (prepared weight), peeled and cut into 1cm (½in) cubes
fine salt
groundnut or coconut oil, for frying
70g (2½oz) onions, finely diced
1 garlic clove, very finely chopped
1 green chilli, deseeded and finely chopped
2 lime leaves
30g (1oz) crunchy peanut butter
200ml (6¾fl oz/¾ cup minus 1 tablespoon) can of coconut milk
50g (1¾oz) long grain rice, cooked
50g (1¾oz) blanched unsalted peanuts, lightly crushed
2 tablespoons chopped coriander leaves
1 teaspoon Kecap Manis
1 teaspoon dark soy sauce
juice of 1 lime
pinch of Maldon salt

For the chilli sauce
1 hot red chilli, finely chopped
50ml (1⅔ fl oz/3½ tablespoons) rice vinegar
150ml (5fl oz/⅔ cup) water
50g (1¾oz/¼ cup) caster (superfine) sugar
½ garlic clove, very finely chopped
5cm (2in) piece of fresh ginger, peeled and finely chopped
1 teaspoon cornflour (cornstarch), made into a paste with 1 tablespoon cold water

To finish (optional)
spring onions, finely sliced
red chilli, finely sliced

ALTERNATIVE & CREATIVE PASTRY

○ GF | VE

It is easier to have the filling already made and cooled prior to making the pastry, so do that first.

Very lightly cook the potato cubes in a pan of salted boiling water for 3–4 minutes after the water returns to the boil, then drain. Drizzle a little oil in a warm frying pan, add the onions and sauté until softened, then add the garlic and chilli, gently frying for 3–4 minutes. Add the potato, lime leaves, peanut butter and coconut milk, bring to a simmer and bubble for 2 minutes, until thickened. Stir through the cooked rice, then remove from the heat and allow to cool; the rice will absorb the liquid. When cool, add the crushed peanuts and coriander and season with the Kecap Manis, soy sauce and lime juice. Adjust seasoning to personal taste, however be aware that the finished dish will have extra seasoning, as the flavoursome syrup is added towards the end of baking. Set aside.

Make the pastry following the recipe and stretching instructions on page 30. Cut into 20cm (8in) squares, dust and rub each well with cornflour (cornstarch) and layer up if needs be, covering well to prevent drying out. Continue stretching and cutting the pastry until all of the dough has been used.

To assemble, line the tin with non-stick baking paper. Lay a cut square of sheet pastry into the base, then brush with melted coconut oil. Repeat with three more layers. Place the filling on top, spreading it into the corners and

flattening with the back of a spoon. Top the satay mixture with the remaining sheets of pastry, brushing each layer with coconut oil, as before. Coat the final layer with coconut oil then make 4cm (1½in) vertical incisions into the pastry, cutting right through to the base of the tray. Now cut across diagonally to make small portions.

Preheat the oven to 180°C (350°F), Gas Mark 4. Once it has reached temperature, bake the filled pastry in the oven for 25 minutes.

As the pastry bakes, make the chilli sauce by adding all of the ingredients, except the cornflour (cornstarch) paste, to a small saucepan. Bring to the boil then pour in the paste. Allow to bubble for 2 minutes, stirring, then remove from the heat and set the pan aside. Towards the end of the baking time, reheat the sauce, remove the baking tin from the oven and pour the chilli syrup evenly over the pastry. As the sauce falls into the incisions and hits the base of the tin it may bubble up, so do be careful. Return to the oven for a further 10 minutes until golden.

Allow to cool slightly before removing from the tin. Sprinkle over some sliced spring onions and chilli and serve, cut into pieces.

PISTACHIO TART WITH RHURBARB TILES

I love rhubarb. It has one of those distinct flavours that transports me back to childhood. I've many happy memories of eating overly sweetened rhubarb swamped in custard round at Nana Maud's house, the perfect ending to her epic Sunday roast dinners. This recipe celebrates rhubarb's characteristic tartness rather than disguising it with too much sugar. I've used early forced rhubarb, which is such a treat to use – the beautiful pink to red stems giving a sweeter, more delicate flavour. Sadly, the season is short, but up to late summer you can use later greener rhubarb, which works equally well, although a generous dusting of sugar prior to baking may be needed to balance the sharper taste.

SERVES 9,
using a loose-bottomed, fluted square tin
measuring 23 x 23 x 2.5cm (9 x 9 x 1in)

1 quantity Sweet Shortcrust pastry (see
   page 12)
egg wash (see page 38)

For the frangipane
100g (3½oz/½ cup minus 1 tablespoon)
   unsalted butter, at room temperature
100g (3½oz/½ cup) caster (superfine) sugar,
   plus extra for sprinkling
70g (2½oz) ground pistachios
80g (2¾oz) ground almonds
100g (3½oz) eggs (shelled weight), lightly
   beaten

For the fruit decoration
4–6 rhubarb stems, depending on thickness
4 eating apples – Pink Lady work well
juice of 2 large lemons
8 blackberries or blueberries (optional)

To finish
pastry decorations
100ml (3⅓fl oz/⅓ cup plus 1 tablespoon)
   water
50g (1¾oz/¼ cup) caster (superfine) sugar
½ teaspoon ground ginger
slivered pistachios (optional)

ALTERNATIVE & CREATIVE PASTRY

● GF

Make the pastry following the recipe on page 12. After resting, line, blind bake and trim the pastry case using the tips and method on page 38. Any spare pastry can be cut into shapes and used to make decorations. Keep the baked pastry case in its tin for later use.

For the frangipane, beat together the softened butter and sugar, either by hand or with a freestanding mixer. When combined, add one-third of each of the ground nuts, mix to combine, then add one-third of the eggs, mix to combine, and so on, until all of the ingredients have been added. Be careful not to overmix, as this will introduce too much air into the frangipane, which will have an effect on the finished bake. Half-fill the pastry case with a layer of the frangipane, smoothing it out evenly with a palette knife and place in the fridge while you prepare the fruit.

If decorating the tart as shown, you will need to select rhubarb stems that are similar in width to one another. Carefully slice the rhubarb across each stem into 1cm (½in) thick pieces, trimming the coloured skin off the flat side of half the slices, to expose the white flesh inside (see overleaf). To soften the apples, follow the instructions on page 53, remembering to use the lemon juice.

Remove the tart base from the fridge and start to lay the rhubarb tiles onto the frangipane in a staggered effect – working from adjacent corners, alternating between the red and white

sides of the rhubarb, until most of the frangipane is covered (leave a diagonal strip clear for the extra fruit). Before adding the apples, dry well on a tea towel then place them in a decorative manner along the exposed frangipane. You may not need all of the slices. Add the berries and any pastry decorations you have prepared (remembering to egg wash those). When you are happy with your design, make a sugar syrup by boiling the water, sugar and ground ginger together in a small pan for a few minutes until thickened. Allow to cool for 5 minutes, then brush over the rhubarb and apple. Place in the fridge for at least an hour before baking.

Preheat the oven to 160°C (325°F), Gas Mark 3. Sprinkle the tart with a dusting of sugar before placing it onto a baking sheet. Cover with kitchen foil and place in the oven. The tart can take up to 2 hours to cook, the time depending on how deep the frangipane has been spread, oven accuracy and how thick the fruit has been sliced. I suggest checking after the first hour, then every 20 minutes thereafter, removing the foil for the final 20 minutes. The tart is ready when you can see that the frangipane has dried, leaving the sides of the pastry case, and the fruit is tender.

Remove from the oven and allow the tart to cool before removing from the tin. Sprinkle with pistachio slivers, if using, then slice and serve either warm or cold.

'Artistry aside, what we mustn't forget, is that the fundamental, most important and rewarding aspect of making and baking with pastry, should always be in the eating.'

CHOCOLATE, CHERRY AND ALMOND PITHIVIERS

A pithivier is a free-form French pie made from puff pastry. With no tin used, the filling is enveloped between two discs of pastry, sealed, decorated and baked – truly delicious. They can be both sweet and savoury, the fillings encased as imaginative as you wish. Here I've opted for cherry and chocolate, the cherries working in perfect harmony with the almond frangipane.

MAKES 4 SMALL PITHIVIERS

1 quantity Inverted Puff pastry (see page 20)
flour, for dusting
egg wash (see page 38)

For the cherry jam
125g (4¼oz) cherries, frozen work well
30g (1oz/2½ tablespoons) caster (superfine)
  sugar
juice of ¼ lemon
pinch of salt

For the frangipane
50g (1¾oz/3½ tablespoons) unsalted butter,
  softened
50g (1¾oz/¼ cup) caster (superfine) sugar
50g (1¾oz) ground almonds
50g (1¾oz) eggs, shelled weight, lightly
  beaten
2 teaspoons best-quality cocoa powder
35g (1¼oz) dark chocolate, finely chopped

ALTERNATIVE & CREATIVE PASTRY

● P
○ GF | SH | SW | VIE

Make the pastry following the recipe on page 20. After the final fold, rest in the fridge for at least 1 hour. If the pastry has been made in advance, see notes on page 19 before rolling.

Roll the pastry as instructed on page 22, to a thickness of around 5mm (¼in), doing your best to keep it a rectangular shape. Trim off the very outer edges, cut the pastry in half across the width, then place both pieces back into the fridge until later.

To make the jam, place all of the ingredients in a small saucepan and gently simmer until the sugar dissolves and the fruit releases its juice, after which time increase the heat for a couple of minutes. When it is starting to thicken, reduce to a slow simmer and cook for 20 minutes or so. The juices will become jammy, coating the back of a spoon easily. When done, transfer to a bowl and allow to cool completely before storing in the fridge.

To make the frangipane, beat the soft butter and caster (superfine) sugar in a mixing bowl with a wooden spoon until light and fluffy. Add the nuts and eggs alternately in three consecutive bursts, beating continuously between additions. Add the cocoa powder and chopped chocolate and give a final, yet brief, mix. Place in the fridge until cold.

Retrieve the pastry and fillings from the fridge. Onto one half of the pastry, gently mark four circles using a 9cm (3½in) pastry cutter. In the centre of the marked circles, place 1 tablespoon of the chocolate frangipane and make a well in the centre, then add a teaspoon

of the jam. Brush the exposed pastry border between the frangipane and the marked circle with egg wash.

Place the remaining pastry half over the top of the bases, matching up the edges, and use cupped hands to seal bottom to top well. Position the same 9cm (3½in) pastry cutter so that the mound of filling is in the centre, then cut through the pastry using a sharp and swift movement (this helps the layers to rise well). Repeat with the remaining three mounds. Freeze for 20 minutes, then gently score a decorative pattern across the top of each using a sharp knife.

Preheat the oven to 180°C (350°F), Gas Mark 4. Using the remaining egg wash, brush the surface of each pithivier evenly, not letting any run down the cut sides. Line the pithiviers on a baking tray evenly, leaving room between each to allow for expansion, then lay a sheet of non-stick baking paper over the top. Place a lightweight ovenproof/baking tray on top (the base of a loose-bottomed baking tin is perfect for this), then bake under the weight for 25 minutes. If the rise seems uneven or if the weight gets pushed off – the 'puff' can be forceful – correct this by either pushing the mini pies back into shape, or replacing the weight. After 25 minutes remove the weight and continue to bake for a further 10–15 minutes, until the layers are set and the pastry is crisp.

Allow to cool before serving – my preference is to eat these cold with an extra dollop of the jam.

CHOCOLATE, PECAN AND BRAZIL NUT BARS

Pecan pie isn't something that is regularly seen or baked here in Cumbria, I had never even tasted it until in my late 30s. Crazy, I know, given that pecans are one of my favourite nuts, those and Brazil nuts – hence the latter's rather unconventional appearance within these bars, though other nuts such as peanuts, cashews or macadamia would work well, too. Of course, this recipe can be set into a round tart tin and served as a more conventional pie, but I rather like the portion given when sliced into bars.

SERVES 12,
using a loose-bottomed 18 x 2.5cm (7 x 1in) square tin

½ quantity Sweet Shortcrust pastry (see page 12)

For the filling
25g (¾oz/1½ tablespoons) salted butter
50g (1¾oz) golden syrup
40g (1½oz) maple syrup
50g (1¾oz) dark chocolate, broken into chunks
50g (1¾oz/¼ cup) soft light brown sugar
1 teaspoon vanilla bean paste (optional)
1 tablespoon plain (all-purpose) flour
2 eggs
100g (3½oz) whole pecan nuts, toasted – 24 left whole, the remainder chopped
60g (2oz) Brazil nuts, toasted and chopped

ALTERNATIVE & CREATIVE PASTRY

○ SH | VIE
● GF

Make the pastry following the recipe on page 12. After resting, line, blind bake and trim a pastry case, using the tips and method on page 38. Keep the pastry case in the tin until needed.

Preheat the oven to 150°C (300°F), Gas Mark 2. Meanwhile make the filling. Set a heatproof bowl on top of a pan of simmering water, making sure that the base of the bowl isn't touching the water, and add the butter, syrups, chocolate and sugar to it. Let the rising heat slowly melt everything together, stirring every so often. Remove from the heat then stir through the vanilla and flour, then add the eggs – one at a time, giving a good stir in between each addition. Tip in the chopped nuts, give one final mix and pour into the pre-baked pastry case. Top decoratively with the whole pecans.

Bake in the oven for 25 minutes. When done the filling should have a slight wobble towards the centre, which sets fully when cooling. If needed, bake for longer, checking again after 5 minutes.

Allow to cool completely before removing from the tin. Slice the very ends from two adjacent sides and slice equally into bars. Those could then be halved or quartered for a smaller portions, or if you are hungry, leave them as is!

CHAPTER 5

Vegetables

VEGETABLE PATCH(WORK) TART

This savoury tart can be made using a variety of vegetables; any that lend themselves well to being cut into rounds, and ones that hold their shape when cooked. Using different-coloured vegetables to create the patchwork effect not only looks attractive, the variety of flavour and nutrients present in coloured vegetables make this tart appealing in more ways than one.

SERVES 6–8

1 quantity Puff pastry (see page 16)
egg wash (see page 38)

For the purée

1kg (2¼lbs) butternut squash, cut into large chunks (no need to peel), seeds discarded
3 banana shallots, halved lengthways and skin on
3 whole garlic cloves, skin on
1 teaspoon fennel seeds
Maldon salt and black pepper
1 tablespoon thyme leaves, plus extra to finish
olive oil, for drizzling
80g (3oz/⅓ cup plus 1 teaspoon) salted butter, to finish

For the patchwork – a selection of the below cut into 5 x 3cm (2 x 1¼in) discs

baking potato
sweet potato
celeriac
swede
butternut squash
beetroot

ALTERNATIVE & CREATIVE PASTRY

● GF | P | S
○ SH

Make the pastry following the recipe on page 16. After the final fold, rest in the fridge for at least 1 hour. If the pastry has been made further in advance, see page 38 before rolling.

Preheat the oven to 180°C (350°F), Gas Mark 4. I like to blind bake this tart, ensuring beautiful, crisp, buttery layers. Roll the whole batch of pastry into a rectangular shape approximately 5mm (¼in) in thickness. Trim the very outer edges and lay on a large baking sheet lined with non-stick baking paper. Place a second sheet of non-stick baking paper on top of the pastry and top with another baking sheet. Bake, with the tray on top of the pastry, for 30 minutes. After this time, remove the top tray and paper and return to the oven for a further 5–10 minutes until deep golden. Remove from the oven and slide the pastry, along with the baking paper underneath, onto a wire rack.

In the meantime, make the purée. Add the squash, shallots, garlic, seasonings and thyme to a deep roasting tray, tucking the shallots and garlic amongst the squash so they don't burn. Drizzle well with olive oil and roast, uncovered, for 40 minutes, stirring halfway through. When the vegetables are softening and taking on colour, cover with kitchen foil and roast for a further 40 minutes. Allow to cool. Remove the skin from both the squash and shallots and pop the flesh from the skins of each garlic clove. Place everything in a food processor, along with any oil and seasonings from the roasting tray.

Heat the butter in a small saucepan until it froths and browns. Remove the

browned butter from the heat, pour into a small bowl through a fine sieve, and reserve. Allow to cool before adding three-quarters of this to the roasted vegetables, then purée in the processor. Place in the fridge until needed.

Blanch the prepared vegetable discs in a pan of salted boiling water for no more than 2 minutes, then drain. If using beetroot, blanch this separately, to avoid the other vegetables from becoming tainted with its colour.

Select a baking tray or tin in which to finish the tart. Here I have used a loose-bottomed, rectangular fluted tart tin, measuring 28 x 18 x 3cm (11 x 7 x 1¼in). Using the base of the tin as a guide, trim the pastry rectangle to size and place into the tin. Reserve the trimmed pastry.

Generously spread the butternut squash purée over the pastry case, then lay the reserved pastry trimmings to create a border, facing them on their side to show off the layers. Spread the purée across the bottom in an even layer and arrange the blanched vegetables in an alternating patchwork fashion on top.

Preheat the oven to 140°C (275°F), Gas Mark 1. Brush the vegetables with the remaining browned butter, season and sprinkle with extra thyme leaves, then bake for 20 minutes or until the vegetables are hot and starting to colour around the edges. Cover the pastry border with foil towards the end of baking if needs be.

Serve hot with some lemony peas.

CHESTNUT AND MUSHROOM ROTOLO

Rotolo is a delicious rolled pasta dish that originated in Emilia-Romagna, Italy. When making this one afternoon it suddenly dawned on me that this filling would work equally well if rolled in sheet pastry. Upon trying it didn't disappoint, the crispy pastry encasing the soft centre was perfect, the sauce offering an extra hug of comfort. Subsequently I am now hooked on making all things 'rotolo', and not just with pasta.

SERVES 4–6

1 quantity Sheet pastry (see page 30)
60g (2¼oz/¼ cup) salted butter, melted and
    browned
fine salt and black pepper

For the filling

60g (2oz/¼ cup) salted butter
olive oil, for frying
250g (8¾oz) each of chestnut, field and
    white mushrooms, finely sliced
Maldon salt and black pepper
10g (⅓oz) dried porcini, rehydrated in
    300ml (10fl oz/1¼ cups) boiling water
1 large garlic clove, very finely chopped
1 tablespoon chopped thyme leaves
1 tablespoon finely chopped parsley leaves
180g (6⅓oz) vacuum-packed chestnuts,
    chopped

For the sauce

40g (1½oz/3 tablespoons) salted butter
olive oil, for frying
100g (3½oz) white mushrooms, finely sliced
Maldon salt and black pepper
1 large garlic clove, very finely sliced
¼ leek, quartered and finely sliced
400ml (13¾fl oz/1¾ cups minus 1
    tablespoon) chicken or vegetable stock
200ml (6¾fl oz/¾ cup plus 2 tablespoons)
    double (heavy) cream
handful of spinach leaves
1 tablespoon finely chopped fresh parsley
fresh nutmeg, for grating

To garnish (optional)

green leaves, such as chickweed or rocket

ALTERNATIVE & CREATIVE PASTRY

○ CH | GF | HW | S | VIE

As the filling needs to be cold prior to rolling, make this first. Add the butter, along with a splash of olive oil, to a large hot frying pan. Add the sliced fresh mushrooms, season with a good pinch of salt and a grinding of pepper and allow to cook for 20 minutes, stirring every so often. After those 20 minutes, the mushrooms will have released most of their moisture and will have started to fry. Drain the rehydrated porcini through a sieve lined with wet kitchen paper (to catch the grit), reserving the liquid. Rinse the porcini to remove any remaining particles, then finely chop. Add these to the pan along with the garlic, thyme and a little more oil. Continue to cook for a further 5 minutes, stirring now and then. Add the porcini liquid, simmering to evaporate. Stir through the chopped chestnuts, check the seasoning and adjust if necessary. Transfer everything from the pan to a bowl and allow to cool completely.

Make and stretch the sheet pastry over a table or work surface covered with a cloth, as instructed on page 30. When fully stretched, trim to a rectangle measuring approximately 50 x 100cm (20in x 3ft), then brush the whole surface with the browned butter and sprinkle over some fine salt and black pepper. Allow the pastry to dry slightly on the cloth for about an hour.

Preheat the oven to 180°C (350°F), Gas Mark 4. Lay the filling along a shorter edge of the pastry, tucking in the outer sides, thus securing the filling in place for rolling. Roll up, using the cloth underneath to help. Roll fairly tightly until you reach the opposite end of the

pastry, use some of the melted butter as glue. Transfer to a baking sheet lined with non-stick baking paper and position so that the pastry's seam is underneath. Brush with any remaining butter and bake in the oven for 40–45 minutes until crisp and golden.

While the rotolo bakes, make the sauce. Heat a large frying pan, add the butter and a splash of oil. Add the mushrooms, season and fry until turning brown. Add both the garlic and leek and sauté until soft, then add the stock, simmering until the liquid has reduced by half. Pour in the cream, bring back to a simmer and gently bubble for 5 or so minutes until thickened. Add the spinach and parsley, a grating of nutmeg and check the seasoning.

When the rotolo has baked, slice into portions and serve in a puddle of sauce, adding a sprig of greenery to garnish, if so desired.

TRINARY PIE

A pie filling made entirely from shallots may seem strange, but believe me it's quite something. The shallots are cooked three ways and brought together to create a unique and delicious filling – tangy yet creamy and full of umami savouriness. If you love shallots, this pie is for you. The filling is dreamy as is, yet it could be enhanced further to suit a daily craving or personal taste. A layer of creamy goat's cheese would work well, as would the addition of some smoked fried pancetta.

SERVES 4–6,
using a loose-bottomed, fluted 18 x 3cm
(7 x 1¼in) circular tart tin

2 quantities of Salted Shortcrust pastry (see page 10)
egg wash (see page 38)

For the fried shallots
100g (3½oz/½ cup minus 1 tablespoon) salted butter
400g (14oz) banana shallots, peeled, root removed and finely sliced
Maldon salt and black pepper
100ml (3⅓fl oz/⅓ cup plus 1 tablespoon) double (heavy) cream
1 teaspoon chopped rosemary leaves
1 teaspoon mustard (I like Dijon)
2 teaspoons gravy browning (optional)

For the roasted shallots
400g (14oz) larger round shallots
olive oil, for drizzling
rosemary leaves, chopped
30g (1oz/2 tablespoons) salted butter, softened
150ml (5fl oz/⅔ cups) vegetable stock or water

For the pickled shallots
250g (8½oz) small pickling shallots
3 tablespoons olive oil
3 tablespoons caster (superfine) sugar
3 tablespoons quick pickling vinegar (I use Sarson's Pickle in 15)
2 sprigs of tarragon
1 teaspoon dried oregano

ALTERNATIVE & CREATIVE PASTRY

● HW
○ GF | SH | VIE

Make and rest the pastry following the recipe on page 10. After resting, halve the pastry and use one half to line, blind bake and trim a pastry case (see tips and techniques on page 38), leave the baked case in the tin for later. Place the remaining pastry into the fridge, as this will be used to make the pie lid later.

For the fried shallots, melt the butter in a medium saucepan over a low heat. Add the sliced shallots, some salt and pepper, and cook very gently for 30 minutes, stirring occasionally. When the shallots are soft and can be easily squashed between your fingers, add the cream and rosemary. Simmer for 20 minutes. Turn off the heat, stir through the mustard and add the browning, if using, then transfer to a bowl. Leave to cool.

Preheat the oven to 180°C (350°F), Gas Mark 4. To roast the shallots, slice off the very tops of each, but leave the skin on. Select a roasting dish that will fit all of the shallots snugly and arrange them tightly around the dish. Pour a little oil on each, sprinkle with salt and pepper, add some rosemary, then spread the softened butter over. Pour the stock into the dish, then place in the oven and bake for 30 minutes. Take out of the oven, baste with the buttery juices, then return to the oven for a further 30 minutes, or until the flesh has softened and the tops have caramelized. Remove from the oven and allow to cool completely before slipping each shallot from its skin. Set to one side.

To pickle the shallots, bring a pan of water to the boil and submerge the shallots, unpeeled, for 5 minutes. After this time, drain and peel. Place the oil, sugar, vinegar, tarragon and oregano in a saucepan and add the peeled shallots. Cover and simmer for 20 minutes until tender and starting to caramelize – the liquid should thicken to a glaze. Season, then cool. Mix together the fried, roasted and pickled shallots, and use this to fill the pastry case. If any filling remains, use it for another meal.

Use the remaining pastry to create the pie lid, whether covering with a decorative top (as pictured) or leaving plain. Refer to the notes on page 42 on how to transfer the lid to the base, remembering to chill the topped pie for 30 minutes prior to baking.

Preheat the oven to 180°C (350°F), Gas Mark 4. Brush the pie surface evenly with the egg wash, then bake in the oven for 45 minutes, but check it after 30 minutes. If any raised pastry décor is taking on too much colour, cover loosely with kitchen foil until ready.

When the pastry is beautifully golden and crisp, remove from the oven. Allow the pie to cool slightly, then remove from the tin, slice and serve warm, perhaps with some gravy, creamy mash and seasonal greens.

ONION AND EGG TARTLETS

Eggs were one of the first things I learned how to cook, and from a young age I was allowed to make them, unsupervised, to feed the family. I love the simplicity and versatility of a cooked egg; they transform the humblest of meals into a treat, adding a certain luxury thanks to the creaminess of the yolks.

This is such a frugal dish, yet when these inexpensive ingredients are brought together, a little bit of magic happens. I would happily serve these tarts as a starter at a dinner party.

SERVES 6,
using 6 small, loose-bottomed circular 8 x 2.5cm (3¼ x 1in) tartlet tins

1 quantity Salted Gluten-free pastry (see page 32)

For the roasted onions
4 medium-large brown onions, halved horizontally, skins on
olive oil, for drizzling
40g (1½oz/3¼ tablespoons) salted butter, softened
1 teaspoon thyme leaves
Maldon salt and black pepper
200ml (6¾fl oz/¾ cup plus 2 tablespoons) chicken or vegetable stock

For the creamed onions
120g (4¼oz/½ cup plus 1 teaspoon) salted butter
3 large mild onions (approximately 600g/1lb 5oz), finely sliced
Maldon salt and black pepper
180ml (6¼oz/¾ cup plus 1 teaspoon) double (heavy) cream
1 tablespoon thyme leaves

For the eggs
3 eggs, at room temperature

To garnish
juice of ½ lemon
2 tablespoons extra virgin olive oil
fresh pea shoots
chickweed fronds (optional)

ALTERNATIVE & CREATIVE PASTRY

○ HW | S
● CH | P | SH | VIE

Make the pastry following the recipe on page 32. When chilled, line, blind bake and trim 6 tartlet cases. See the tips and techniques on page 38 if needed. Set to one side and allow to cool.

Preheat the oven to 180°C (350°F), Gas Mark 4. To roast the onions, place the halves, cut-side up, in a small roasting tray. Drizzle each with a little oil, then rub over the butter. Sprinkle with the thyme, add some salt and pepper and pour the stock into the tray. Roast in the oven for 1½ hours, basting at intervals. Allow to cool before slipping the onions from their skins, then separate them into rings and transfer to a clean pan. Pour over the roasting juices and set to one side.

While they are roasting, make the creamed onions. First, melt the butter in a saucepan and add the sliced onions along with some salt and pepper. Allow to very slowly cook for 40 minutes, stirring frequently – they will become lightly golden and melting. Don't rush the process, it's the slow cooking that makes them so delicious. After 40 minutes, pour in the cream and add the thyme. Allow to simmer for a further 20 minutes, stirring occasionally. Switch off the heat, but leave in the pan until needed.

These tarts are best served warm, so have everything warming while boiling the eggs. The pastry cases can be warmed in a very low oven, and the onions in their pans doing the same. Have the salad garnish ready and dressed with the oil and lemon juice.

Boil the kettle. Place the eggs in a saucepan and pour in the boiled water, making sure the stream of water doesn't hit the eggs directly (they may crack). Bring the water back to the boil and time exactly 4 minutes. When done, drain the eggs and set under cold running water for 1 minute. Once cool enough to handle, carefully peel each egg, then halve each.

Assemble the tartlets by spooning a layer of the creamed onions into each tartlet case, then top with a generous amount of roasted onions, drizzling over any roasting juices. Top each tartlet with an egg half and add a small amount of dressed salad garnish to each. Finish with a sprinkling of salt and pepper and serve immediately.

GRIDDLED GREENS, CAULIFLOWER AND LEMON TRIANGLES

The green vegetables within these triangles can be changed as the seasons pass. Asparagus and broad beans are my favourite, however, all of the long beans work well, as do fresh peas and Chinese cabbage. Really, the recipe is open for variation, as pretty much any vegetable would work. The triangles can also be baked if frying isn't your thing, but if you do so, it is worth noting that the fresh taste of the vegetables will be lost somewhat, due to the longer cooking time required to crisp the pastry.

MAKES 10–12

1 quantity Sheet pastry (see page 30)
cornflour (cornstarch), for dusting
vegetable oil, for brushing
fine salt and pepper

For the filling

2 courgettes, thinly sliced, lengthways
4–6 asparagus spears, halved lengthways
oil, for griddling
100g (3½oz) broad beans, fresh or frozen
100g (3½oz) cauliflower florets, coarsely
    grated
2 spring onions, finely sliced
juice of 1 lemon
1 tablespoon peppery olive oil
Maldon salt and black pepper
½ teaspoon poppy seeds
½ teaspoon chia seeds
¼ teaspoon dried chilli flakes (optional)
2 tablespoons finely chopped fresh
    parsley leaves

For griddling and finishing

500ml (17fl oz/2 cups plus 2 tablespoons)
    vegetable oil, for griddling
chia seeds (optional)
lemon wedges, to serve

Yoghurt dip (optional)

200ml (6¾fl oz/¾ cup plus 2 tablespoons)
    natural yoghurt
juice of 1 lemon
1 tablespoon fresh mint, leaves chopped
1 tablespoon parsley, leaves chopped
1 teaspoon chia seeds
Maldon salt and black pepper

ALTERNATIVE & CREATIVE PASTRY

○ GF | P | S | VE | VIE

As the filling needs to be cold before use, make this first. Char the courgette slices and asparagus halves by griddling them in a hot pan brushed with oil, then chop into small pieces and place in a large bowl. In a pan of boiling salted water, blanch the broad beans for 2 minutes then plunge them straight into iced water. Add the grated cauliflower to the boiling water and cook until soft – this should only take a minute or two. Drain, and add to the courgettes and asparagus.

I prefer to remove the thick skin from broad beans, but this is optional and a stage you might wish to skip. Either way, add the broad beans (skinned or not) to the other vegetables along with the spring onions. Mix in both the lemon juice and olive oil and season well with salt and pepper. Add the poppy and chia seeds, chilli flakes and parsley, check the seasoning and adjust if necessary. Leave to cool.

Make, rest and stretch the sheet pastry (see tips and techniques on page 30), then cut into long rectangles measuring 10 x 30cm (4 x 12in). Dust and rub the pieces with cornflour (cornstarch), then cover with cling film until needed (though don't make it too far in advance). Assemble the pastries, one at a time, and always keep the remaining sheet pastry covered while you do so, to prevent drying.

To assemble the triangles, position a pastry rectangle with a shorter side closest to you. Spoon some of the vegetable mixture onto the bottom left-hand corner, then flip the pastry over until the edges line up. Flip over six more times, creating a triangle. Secure the loose end with a little oil, then rest upon a tray lined with non-stick baking paper. Repeat until all of the pastry has been used. If any vegetable mixture remains, simply eat alongside the finished dish as a salad.

Heat the vegetable oil to 180°C (350°F), either in a suitable pan or deep-fat fryer. Ensure that the oil has reached the required temperature prior to frying so that the pastry cooks and turns golden quickly, keeping the vegetables inside as fresh-tasting as possible. Deep-fry the pastries in batches until the pastry is golden and beautifully crisp, about 3–4 minutes turning halfway, then drain on kitchen paper. Keep warm until the rest of the pastries have been deep-fried. Sprinkle with salt, pepper and chia seeds (if using) while still hot.

To make the dipping yoghurt, if using, simply mix all of the ingredients together in a bowl, seasoning well.

Serve the pastries immediately, with lemon wedges for squeezing over.

CELERIAC AND APPLE TARTE FINES

Celeriac is one of my favourite vegetables, with its unique and comforting flavour. I use it in many dishes, boiled for use in soups and purées, roasted in gratins, fried in rösti, even pickled or, like here, raw. It truly is a versatile veg, which thankfully seems to be having its turn in the popularity stakes. Due to the mild and creamy nature of celeriac, it pairs well with many flavours, both savoury and sweet.

MAKES 6 TARTS,
I used an oval cutter measuring
  12.5 x 8cm (4½ x 3in)

1 quantity Salted Gluten-free pastry (see
  page 32)
cornflour (cornstarch), for dusting

For the apple sauce
4 eating apples, peeled, cored and chopped
2 tablespoons caster sugar
100ml (3⅓fl oz/⅓ cup plus 1 tablespoon)
  water
4–6 teaspoons horseradish cream,
  depending on personal taste

For the salad
juice of 1 lemon
½ small celeriac, peeled
2 red-skinned dessert apples, cored
seeds of ½ large pomegranate
1 celery stalk, strings removed, sliced
6 radishes, finely sliced
handful of fresh tarragon, chopped
edible flower petals (optional)
green salad leaves of choice – I have used
  chickweed, tagetes and yarrow
fresh horseradish root (if available), peeled
handful of fresh herbs, to serve

For the dressing
3 tablespoons olive oil
2 teaspoons pomegranate molasses
1 teaspoon red wine vinegar
Maldon salt and black pepper

ALTERNATIVE & CREATIVE PASTRY

● HW | IP | S | VE
○ CH | P | SH | VIE

Make the pastry following the recipe on page 32. Roll it out between two sheets of non-stick baking paper to around 5mm (¼in) depth – you might need a dusting of cornflour (cornstarch). Return to the fridge for at least 30 minutes.

Preheat the oven to 180°C (350°F), Gas Mark 4. Line a baking sheet with non-stick baking paper.

Cut six ovals (or your desired shape) from the pastry sheet and lay them on the lined baking sheet, then bake in the oven for 25 minutes. The pastry is ready when it is both golden and crisp. Remove from the oven and allow to cool on a wire rack.

To make the apple sauce, simply place the apples, sugar and water into a small saucepan and gently cook until the apples are soft and collapsing. Allow to cool, then whizz to a purée in a food processor or mush by hand with a fork, adding a splash of water to loosen, if needed. Stir through the horseradish, then set to one side. This amount will make more than you need, so I suggest serving the rest alongside the Slow-Braised Pork Cheek and Mushroom Pie on page 168.

Prepare the salad. Add the lemon juice to a bowl of water. Prepare the celeriac by slicing and cutting it very finely into matchsticks. Do the same with the apples, but leave the skin on for the colour. Place both into the bowl of lemon water to prevent them turning brown.

Put the pomegranate seeds into a bowl with the sliced celery and radishes, along with the chopped tarragon, flower petals (if using) and picked salad leaves. Grate in a little horseradish, if using, then season well with salt and pepper. Just before serving, drain the celeriac and apple matchsticks, pat dry with kitchen paper and add to the rest of the salad. Toss to mix.

Prepare the dressing by mixing everything together, adding salt and pepper to taste. When ready to assemble, place a pastry base onto each plate and either spread or pipe some of the apple sauce onto each. Dress the salad lightly and use to top the pastry ovals. Finish with a flurry of fresh herbs and an extra drizzling of dressing.

Fresh, delicate and super pretty.

LEEK, POTATO AND CHEDDAR CHEESE CUBES

These cubed pies should be eaten soon after they are baked, when the creamy sauce is oozing and the filling is warm and soothing. You can change the Cheddar you use to suit personal preference, but I do think a strong cheese is needed. Here I have used a special farmhouse Cheddar from Somerset, the flavour of which is nutty yet fruity, adding a vigorous depth of flavour and an unquestionable richness to the pies.

While I have shown varying sizes of pies for inspiration, this recipe will make 6 small pies using 6.5cm (2½in) cubed metal moulds

1 quantity Hot Water pastry (see page 14) – using all-butter if preferred
plain (all-purpose) flour, for dusting the pie moulds
egg wash (see page 38)

For the filling
50g (1¾oz/3½ tablespoons) salted butter, plus extra for greasing tins
200g (7oz) onions, finely sliced
200g (7oz) leeks, trimmed, washed and finely sliced
1 tablespoon thyme leaves
Maldon salt and black pepper
300g (10½oz) waxy potatoes, washed, quartered and sliced to ½cm
250ml (9fl oz/1 cup plus 1 tablespoon) vegetable stock

For the sauce
50g (1¾oz/3½ tablespoons) salted butter
2 tablespoons plain (all-purpose) flour, plus extra for dusting tins
100ml (3⅓fl oz/⅓ cup plus 1 tablespoon) vegetable stock
100ml (3⅓fl oz/⅓ cup plus 1 tablespoon) milk
160g (5¾oz) Keen's Farmhouse Cheddar, grated
black pepper

ALTERNATIVE & CREATIVE PASTRY

○ GF | S | SH | VIE

Make the pastry following the recipe on page 14, up to and including the fridge resting. Leave in the fridge for up to 1 hour while making the filling.

Heat a large sauté pan and add the butter, onions, leeks, thyme and a good pinch of salt. Allow to cook slowly until soft and just starting to turn golden – this should take around 30 minutes. Add the potatoes with a generous grinding of pepper, stir to combine, then add the stock. Allow to simmer until the potatoes are soft and the liquid has evaporated. Remove from the heat.

To make the sauce, add the butter and flour to a saucepan. Allow the butter to melt and the flour to sizzle for a couple of minutes, then pour in both the stock and milk, whisking continuously until thickened. Allow the sauce to bubble over a low heat for 5 minutes before adding the cheese. Taste and add some pepper if needed, then pour onto the potato mixture. Allow to cool.

Butter and flour the pie moulds and have a baking sheet ready, lined with non-stick baking paper. Roll out the chilled pastry on a lightly floured surface to around 3mm (⅛in) depth. Using one of the moulds, cut out 12 squares – six for the bases, six for the tops (see note *). Now cut six long strips 6.5cm (2½in) wide and 26cm (10½in) in length. These will be the pie walls. Chill the pastry in the fridge for 30 minutes.

Remove the pastry from the fridge and place all the moulds on a baking sheet lined with non-stick baking paper. Lay a pastry base inside each mould, pushing the pastry out to meet the sides, then

brush the outer edges with egg wash. Ease in one pastry strip per pie, then secure the sides to the base. Push down firmly to seal, then push the pastry into all of the edges and up the sides of the mould. As an extra leakproof precaution, roll a thin strip of pastry to push into all of the seams, using a floured finger and more egg wash to secure in place. Return to the fridge for at least 30 minutes.

Fill the pie cases almost to the top with the cooled filling. Brush the very tops of the exposed pastry sides with egg wash and top each with a pre-cut pastry lid. Press to secure tightly. Add a steam hole, then egg wash the surface of each pie carefully. Chill for a minimum of 30 minutes in the fridge.

Preheat the oven to 180°C (350°F), Gas Mark 4. Bake the pies in the oven for 40 minutes. Slip the mould from each pie, egg wash all sides and return to the oven for a further 10–15 minutes, or until the pies are dark golden and crisp.

Allow to cool for 10 minutes before eating. If you are looking for an accompaniment, I'd suggest pickles, chutneys and the like.

*If you want to make the lattice tops, as shown here, pass rolled-out lengths of pastry first through the widest setting of a plain pasta roller and then through a tagliatelle cutter. Use these strips to lay a lattice onto a thinly rolled piece of pastry. Laying directly onto the pastry will act as a platform for the lattice, which can then be chilled and cut to size and easily transferred to the tops of the pies, as described.

Leek
alliums

Drumstick
alliums

SPINACH 'FIGURA DI OTTO'

Spinach with cheese is a classic combination, a pairing used widely across most Mediterranean countries. Think of Italian stuffed pasta, Greek filo pies and the fried borek of the Middle East. I've drawn inspirations from all here, creating a filling that is both sweet, crunchy, creamy and tangy.

I really do enjoy this pastry dish, from stretching the dough, through to shaping and, of course, eating, it is a very soothing and satisfying way to feed your family. I hope you enjoy it, too. Slow-roasted tomatoes, crispy roast potatoes and a lemony salad make for perfect accompaniments.

SERVES 6–8

1 quantity Sheet pastry (see page 30)
60g (2oz/¼ cup) salted butter, melted and browned
fine salt and black pepper

For the filling
3 tablespoons olive oil
500g (18oz) baby spinach, washed and drained and stalks removed
Maldon salt and pepper
1 large garlic clove, very finely sliced
200g (7oz) feta cheese, crumbled
180g (6¼oz) Innes goat's curd, or other variety
50g (1¾oz) golden sultanas, soaked in boiling water
50g (1¾oz) pine nuts, toasted
1 teaspoon dried oregano
2 tablespoons finely chopped parsley leaves
1 tablespoon finely chopped mint leaves
fresh nutmeg, for grating
dried chilli flakes (optional)

To finish
Poppy seeds (optional)

ALTERNATIVE & CREATIVE PASTRY
○ GF | HW | S | VIE

Make and stretch the pastry as instructed on page 30. Trim the pastry and leave as one large sheet measuring 50 x 100cm (20in x 3ft) – small holes or tears won't matter too much.

Brush the whole surface with the browned butter, then sprinkle over some salt and black pepper.

While the pastry dries a little, make the filling. Gently heat a little of the olive oil in a large saucepan and add all of the spinach, season with a good pinch of salt and a grinding of pepper and allow to wilt for a couple of minutes, flipping and moving the spinach in the pan with some kitchen tongs. When done, add the finely sliced garlic and allow to cook for a minute or two until the garlic slithers become opaque. Remove and leave to drain through a colander.

Mix together the cheeses in a bowl. Drain the sultanas, drying well, then add these, along with the pine nuts, dried oregano and fresh herbs to the cheese. Grate in some nutmeg, add a good pinch of salt and pepper, loosen with the remaining olive oil and throw in some dried chilli flakes if you like. Squeeze the spinach to remove any excess moisture, then lay it on a chopping board and roughly chop. Stir into the cheese mix.

Preheat the oven to 180°C (350°F), Gas Mark 4. Along one of the longest sides, lay the filling in one long continuous row. Tuck in the outer shorter edges,

securing everything in place, then start to roll up, using the cloth underneath to help. Roll fairly tightly until the opposite end of the pastry is reached – the melted butter that's already in place will act as a glue, securing all ends. Position so that the seam is underneath, then bring one end round in a swirl, working towards the centre. In the opposite direction, swirl the other end – making a figure of eight, of sorts.

Transfer to a baking sheet lined with non-stick baking paper and brush with any remaining butter. Sprinkle with poppy seeds, if you like, and bake in the oven for 40 minutes, or until beautifully golden and crisp.

Slice into wedges and serve hot.

VEGETABLE WELLINGTON

This is a wow dish, and a great way to celebrate both vegetables and homemade pastry. It's a veggie pie for an occasion and a great alternative to meat and fish. Most vegetables would work well here, so choose your favourites.

For the photograph opposite we used a mixture of pastries, simply because I had a variety of leftovers; the vegetables were first rolled in puff pastry, then finished with a lattice made from hot water pastry. It shows the versatility of this dish, so do go ahead and use whatever pastry you like most or have already made!

SERVES 6

1 quantity Puff pastry (see page 16)
egg wash (see page 38)

For the mushroom layer
50g (1¾oz/3½ tablespoons) salted butter
100g (3½oz) each of chestnut, field and
    white mushrooms, finely sliced
olive oil, for cooking
Maldon salt and black pepper
10g (¼oz) dried porcini, rehydrated in 300ml
    (10fl oz/1¼ cups) boiling water
1 large banana shallot, finely diced
1 garlic clove, finely chopped
1 tablespoon thyme leaves

For the filling (an example)
8 green cabbage leaves, any variety
3 carrots, peeled and cut into batons
6 runner beans, topped and tailed, string
    removed
6 green beans, trimmed
4 asparagus spears, tough ends removed
¼ swede, peeled and cut into batons
1 large baking potato, peeled and cut into
    batons
Maldon salt and black pepper

ALTERNATIVE & CREATIVE PASTRY

● HW | IP | S
○ SH

Make the pastry following the recipe on page 16. After the final fold, rest in the fridge for at least 1 hour. If the pastry has been made further in advance, see notes on page 19 before rolling.

Roll out the puff pastry to 3mm (⅛in) depth and cut a rectangle, measuring approximately 20 x 25cm (8 x 10in) from it. Place it on a baking tray lined with non-stick baking paper, cover and return to the fridge – the leftover pastry can be used for garnishing later.

Add the butter and sliced mushrooms to a pan with a splash of olive oil, season with salt and pepper and allow to cook for 20 minutes, stirring every so often. Drain the porcini through a fine sieve lined with kitchen paper to remove the grit, reserving the liquid, then rinse again, drain and finely chop. Add to the mushroom pan along with the shallot, garlic, thyme and a little more oil, if needed. Continue to cook for 8 minutes, stirring now and then. Add the porcini liquid and simmer until it evaporates. Remove everything from the pan, allow to cool completely, then finely chop.

While the mushrooms are cooking, blanch the vegetables. Have a large pan of salted water boiling, and next to it a large bowl of iced water. Plunge the vegetables into the boiling water, then remove when tender yet still firm when pierced with the tip of a sharp knife (the times vary between varieties of vegetable), then immediately refresh in the iced water. When all the vegetables are cooked and refreshed, drain them, drying them all extremely well on

kitchen paper. Remove the tough middle vein from each cabbage leaf, then sprinkle all the vegetables well with salt and pepper.

Retrieve the pastry rectangle from the fridge and position so that a shorter edge is nearest you. Lay the cabbage leaves on the pastry, overlapping each leaf so there are no gaps between them, but do leave a 2cm (¾in) pastry border clear for sealing. Spread the chopped mushroom mixture over the cabbage then lay and stack all of the other vegetables horizontally over the first third of the area – so the Wellington can be rolled.

Roll the Wellington tightly, finishing so that the seam is underneath. Pinch the pastry at each end, trimming off any excess. Garnish using the remaining pastry – here I have used a sliced lattice effect, which can be done by hand or by using a special cutter. Use the egg wash to secure any décor in place. Return to the fridge for at least 30 minutes.

Preheat the oven to 180°C (350°F), Gas Mark 4. Before baking, use the remaining egg wash to evenly coat the Wellington and then bake it on a baking paper-lined baking sheet for 40–50 minutes, or until the pastry is beautifully golden and crisp, both top and bottom.

Allow to stand for 5 minutes before slicing. As all of the veg is within the pie, I feel that there is no need for further accompaniments other than a decent vegetable-based gravy.

BEETROOT TARTE TATIN

This makes for a wonderful weekend lunch or supper to serve to friends. Serve whole at the table, buffet-style, with a big bowl of interesting salad leaves, some creamy goat's cheese and a chilled bottle of Albariño to accompany. Very lovely indeed.

SERVES 4–6,
using a 20 x 5cm (8 x 2in) tarte tatin dish

1 quantity Puff pastry (see page 16)
egg wash (see page 38)

For the filling
6–8 beetroots, depending on size
fine salt, for seasoning water
3 red onions, each cut into eight, root left
  intact, skin removed
olive oil, for roasting and dressing
Maldon salt and black pepper
1 teaspoon dried oregano
½ teaspoon nigella seeds
2 garlic cloves, skin on

For the caramel
2 tablespoons soft light brown sugar
2 tablespoons pomegranate molasses
30ml (1fl oz/⅛ cup) rice wine vinegar
30ml (1fl oz/⅛ cup) water

ALTERNATIVE & CREATIVE PASTRY

● GF | HW | IP | S | SH | VE

Make the pastry following the recipe on page 16. After the final fold, rest in the fridge for at least 1 hour. If the pastry has been made further in advance, see the notes on page 19 before rolling.

Roll out the pastry to 5mm (¼in) depth and cut a circle from it, 1cm (½in) larger than the dish being used. Rest upon a baking sheet lined with non-stick baking paper and put in the fridge until needed. Do save any extra pastry for another use.

Preheat the oven to 180°C (350°F), Gas Mark 4. Cut a circle of non-stick baking paper to snugly fit the bottom of the tarte tatin dish and place it inside.

Peel the beetroots and cook in a pan of seasoned boiling water until just tender, approximately 20 minutes (size depending) – check with the tip of a sharp knife. When done, drain, cool and cut into equal-sized pieces – quarters or eighths depending on size. Meanwhile, place the onions in a roasting tray and coat lightly with olive oil. Season with salt and pepper and sprinkle with dried oregano and nigella seeds – shake the tin so that all the wedges are coated in the flavourings. Wrap the garlic cloves in some kitchen foil, pouring in a few drops of oil and adding a little salt before sealing. Add this to the roasting tray and place in the oven for 25–35 minutes until the onions soften and are colouring a touch, and the garlic is softening within the foil.

When done, drain the onions on kitchen paper. Remove the garlic from the foil and slip the cloves from their papery skin. Smooth the garlic to a paste using the back of a spoon, then add to a bowl along with the beetroot and onions. Season well and mix everything together, then allow to cool while making the caramel.

Add the sugar, molasses, vinegar and water to a frying pan and stir until the sugar dissolves over a medium heat. When the sugar has dissolved, keep a close eye on the liquid, but do not stir. As the sugar starts to caramelize, swirl the contents of the pan around so that it cooks evenly. When the liquid has thickened and seems sticky, pour it into the pre-lined dish. Leave to cool for a few minutes, then arrange the prepared onions and beetroot snugly around the dish. Top with the chilled pastry disc, tucking in all of the edges between the veg and the dish sides using the back of a spoon, or similar.

Brush the pastry with the egg wash. Pierce the pastry lid once to make a small steam hole, then bake in the oven for 40 minutes, after which time the pastry will have risen and should be beautifully golden.

Remove from the oven, allow to cool in the dish for 10 minutes before inverting onto a plate. Remove the paper disc and serve.

CHAPTER 6

Meat & Fish

CHICKEN, CHORIZO AND SPINACH PIE

Roasting a whole chicken instead of using only the required individual cuts for this recipe is very beneficial. By doing so you'll have tastier, moister chicken meat with the added bonus of having the roasting juices to add back to the sauce, which will enhance the flavour. Any leftover meat can be used for another meal, which is advantageous and cost-effective. Chorizo proves to be a perfect partner here, providing depth of flavour and welcome smokiness.

Serve a generous wedge of pie per person, along with some lightly steamed greens tossed with best-quality extra virgin olive oil, lemon juice and salt flakes.

SERVES 6,
using a loose-bottomed fluted 23 x 3.5cm
  (9 x 1½in) circular tin

2 quantities Salted Shortcrust pastry (see page 10)
egg wash (see page 38)

For the filling
1 medium chicken
olive oil, for roasting
Maldon salt and black pepper
150g (5⅓oz) dry cured chorizo, halved, skin removed and cut into 1cm (½in) slices
200g (7oz) finely sliced onions
1 large garlic clove, finely sliced
60g (2oz) baby spinach, any tough stalks removed

For the sauce
30g (1oz/2 tablespoons) salted butter
3 tablespoons plain (all-purpose) flour
reduced chicken juices (from roasting chicken)
300ml (10fl oz/1¼ cups) milk
3 teaspoons wholegrain mustard

ALTERNATIVE & CREATIVE PASTRY

● HW
○ GF | SH

Make the pastry following the recipe on page 10. After resting, use one half of the pastry to line, blind bake and trim a pastry case – see tips and techniques on page 38. Leave the pastry case in the tin until needed. Place the remaining pastry in the fridge. Preheat the oven to 180°C (350°F), Gas Mark 4.

Place the chicken in a roasting tin and cover with a good drizzle of olive oil followed by a generous sprinkling of salt and grinding of black pepper. Roast for 1¼ hours, basting twice during the cooking time. When fully cooked, remove the chicken from the oven and allow to cool and rest in the roasting tin for 1 hour. Remove the chicken from the tin, reserving all the juices. Skim and discard the fat from the juices in the roasting tin then place the tin over a high heat and allow the juices to reduce to one-third.

Remove one of the breasts, both legs and the oysters from underneath the chicken. The rest of the meat, along with the carcass and skin, can be used for another meal. Dice the leg and breast meat into 2cm (¾in) pieces and place in a bowl along with the chicken oysters, then set aside.

Add the chorizo to a cold frying pan and cook over a low heat, stirring occasionally. Allow the fat to slowly melt from the sausage, the slices turning golden brown – this should take 15 minutes or so. Using a slotted spoon, remove and set on kitchen paper. Add the onions and garlic to the chorizo fat,

season with salt and pepper, cover and cook over a low heat for 20 minutes, stirring occasionally. Drain any excess fat from the onions.

In the meantime, start making the sauce. Melt the butter in a saucepan, then add the flour and stir until thick. Then add the reduced chicken juices and whisk together. Pour in the milk, whisking to avoid lumps and allow to simmer for a few minutes, then stir in the mustard.

Add the drained onions and chorizo to the chicken and pour over the sauce, stirring well to combine. Check for seasoning, adjusting if necessary. Finally, stir in the spinach leaves and allow to cool.

Fill the prepared pastry case with the chilled filling and use the remaining pastry to create the pie lid, whether covering with a decorative top (as pictured) or leaving plain. Refer to the notes on page 42 for how to transfer the lid to the base successfully. Remember to chill the topped pie in the fridge for 30 minutes prior to baking.

Preheat the oven to 180°C (350°F), Gas Mark 4. Carefully brush the pie lid with egg wash. Bake in the oven for 45 minutes, or until the pastry is golden and crisp and the filling is piping hot.

Allow to cool slightly before removing from the tin and slicing to serve.

OXTAIL SCRUNCH POT PIE

Typically, a filling like this would be found inside a suet pudding – soft and yielding. However upon experimenting, I found this pie filling to be most versatile; working well with all encasing pastries, and the added texture from a more structured pastry is an added bonus. Eventually I settled on sheet pastry, the textural contrast between soft and fatty, crisp and crunchy is really quite something.

I would suggest making both the filling and pastry the day before you want to eat this pie – the meat requires a long slow braise and the sauce needs time to reduce. The scrunch topping will also benefit from being air-dried overnight, prior to baking.

There will be enough filling to make two small pies. I always make at least double what is needed when a lengthy cooking time is required, as it seems to justify the amount of energy needed to heat the simmering pot. Simply freeze what is not used, make an extra or larger pie, or turn it into another meal – this filling will work in lots of other dishes, too, think cottage pie or pasta ragu.

SERVES 4–6,
using a 18 x 4cm (7 x 1½in) circular pie
  dish and a circular loose-bottomed 18 x
  3cm (7 x 1¼in) tart case

1 quantity Sheet pastry (see page 30)
50g (1¾oz/3½ tablespoons) salted butter, melted
fine salt and black pepper

For the filling

1kg (2¼lbs) oxtail, cut into sections
300g (10½oz) beef shin, thickly sliced
Maldon salt and black pepper
vegetable oil, for frying
200g (7oz) button mushrooms, thinly sliced
100g (3½oz) carrots, thinly sliced
100g (3½oz) celery stalks, thinly sliced
200g (7oz) onions, thinly sliced
1 tablespoon picked thyme leaves
1 star anise
200ml (6¾fl oz/¾ cup plus 2 tablespoons)
  red wine
750ml (25⅓fl oz/3¼ cups) chicken stock
750ml (25⅓fl oz/3¼ cups) beef stock
400g (14oz) can of chopped tomatoes
1 teaspoon double concentrated tomato
  purée
2 small dried bay leaves

ALTERNATIVE & CREATIVE PASTRY

○ CH | GF | HW | IP | P | S | VIE

Start with the filling. Season the meats with salt and pepper and brown all pieces well in a large, hot pan with some oil. Do this in batches so that the meat fries and browns rather than stews. When browned, transfer the meat to a plate. Add the mushrooms to the same pan, season and fry, stirring occasionally until they too take on a caramel colour. Remove from the pan and drain on kitchen paper. Fry the carrots, celery and onions in a little more oil, add some seasoning, the thyme and star anise and fry until soft and starting to colour. Remove from the pan and drain with the mushrooms.

Deglaze the pan with the red wine and simmer until reduced to a third. Put everything into a big pan – the meat, vegetables, stocks, tinned and puréed tomatoes and the bay leaves. Pour in the reduced wine and bring to the boil. Once boiling, top loosely with a piece of non-stick baking paper, reduce to a simmer and continue to cook for 4 hours – checking the levels every so often and topping up with water if the meat becomes exposed.

To test if the meat is done, squeeze between your fingers – if it crumbles easily it is ready. Turn off the heat and allow everything to cool within the pan. When cooled, pass through a colander, reserving all of the stock.

Pick the meat from the oxtail and shred the shin meat. If the meat fibres are quite long, snip them in half with scissors. Discard the star anise and bay leaves along with any bones or pieces of meat that seem overly dry. Add the vegetables back to the meat and refrigerate until needed.

Chill the stock until the fat rises to the top, a good few hours in the fridge, or, if short on time, use the freezer. Skim the fat from the top and discard. Return the stock to the pan and bring to the boil, then reduce to a simmer and reduce the liquid by half, skimming off any impurities that float across the surface. Pass through a fine sieve and place in the fridge until needed. If making only one pie at this point, remember to halve both meat filling and stock, reserving half for another use.

Continued overleaf

Make and stretch the sheet pastry, as instructed on page 30. Small holes and tears won't matter, so don't worry. After stretching and trimming, brush the entire surface with melted butter and sprinkle over some fine salt and pepper. Cut into large squares, approximately 20cm (8in) and allow to dry for up to 3 hours (environment depending). The pastry needs to be stiff enough to hold some shape, yet still pliable enough to manipulate into the mould without breaking too much. Ease and fold the cut pastry in the loose-bottomed tart tin, folding to add height and texture. Allow to dry further, at room temperature, for at least 4 hours or, even better, overnight.

Preheat the oven to 180°C (350°F), Gas Mark 4. Around 15 minutes prior to serving the pie, add the meat filling to a pan along with three-quarters of the required stock. Bring to the boil then simmer until needed. Reheat the reserved stock in a separate pan to use as a gravy. Heat the pie dish in the oven.

Bake the scrunch topping for 5 minutes, then check it – the pastry will bake very quickly because it is so thin and dry. It will most likely need more time. When beautifully golden, remove from the tart tin and, if feeling brave, turn the

pastry over and bake a little longer to crisp up the bottom. This isn't essential, but it is something that I do.

Transfer the filling to the warmed pie dish and top with the crispy pastry. Serve immediately.

Any vegetables would work well to accompany this pie; serve them alongside with a jug of the reserved warmed stock as a gravy.

MY MUM'S 'TATTY POT' PIE

Tatty Pot – more commonly known as Lancashire hot pot – is a favourite of mine. Although born and raised in Cumbria, I was brought up on this dish, and because of it I have always enjoyed fatty meats and cheaper cuts. This is great winter food, for when you are feeling a little under the weather, run down or when you just need a homely plate of comforting food. Traditionally, this would be made in a roasting tray with no pastry case, which, of course, you can do, if preferred. Although you have to admit it does make rather a spectacular pie, and crispy hot water pastry definitely brings something to the dish. It is worth noting, however, that this pie will not slice neatly, as the filling is far too unctuous for it to hold its shape!

SERVES 8,
using a loose-bottomed pie (or cake) tin measuring 20 x 7.5cm (8 x 3in)

½ quantity Hot Water pastry (see page 14)

For the lamb
1kg (2¼lbs) lamb ribs (800g (1¾lbs) lamb breast can be used as an alternative)
Maldon salt and black pepper
60g (2oz/scant ½ cup) plain (all-purpose) flour
olive oil, for frying and greasing
1 large onion, roughly chopped into 1cm (½in) dice
400g (14oz) carrots, peeled and roughly chopped into 1cm (½in) dice
2 star anise
1 fat garlic clove, finely chopped
2 sprigs of rosemary, leaves picked and finely chopped
250ml (8½fl oz/1 cup plus 1 tablespoon) red wine
40g (1½oz) dried red lentils
500ml (17fl oz/2 cups plus 2 tablespoons) lamb stock
2 tablespoons wholegrain mustard
1 tablespoon redcurrant jelly
1 tablespoon Worcestershire sauce
200ml (6¾fl oz/¾ cup plus 2 tablespoons) water
2 slices best-quality black pudding, cut into bite-size pieces
1 tablespoon cornflour (cornstarch), mixed with 2 tablespoons cold water

For the topping
4 large floury potatoes
100g (3½oz/½ cup minus 1 tablespoon) salted butter
Maldon salt and black pepper
thyme leaves, to garnish

ALTERNATIVE & CREATIVE PASTRY
● S

Preheat the oven to 160°C (325°F), Gas Mark 3. Season the lamb well with salt and pepper, dip into the flour to coat and shake off the excess. Add a little oil to a large, hot frying pan set over a high heat and brown each piece of lamb well on all sides. Remove with tongs and drain on kitchen paper.

In the same pan, fry the onion and carrots, along with the star anise, until starting to lightly brown and soften – this should take around 10 minutes. Stir frequently. Add the garlic and rosemary with some more salt and pepper and sauté for a little longer. Transfer everything to a deep-sided roasting tray, along with the browned lamb. Deglaze the frying pan with the red wine, then allow the wine to reduce to a third. Add this to the roasting tray. Sprinkle over the red lentils – the purpose of these, or so my Mum would say, is 'to soak up some of the fat'.

Mix together the lamb stock, mustard, redcurrant jelly and Worcestershire sauce, then pour into the roasting tray, adding the water, too. Cover the tray with kitchen foil and place in the oven for 1½ hours, after which time, remove the foil, give everything a good stir and add the pieces of black pudding. Return to the oven, uncovered this time, for 1 hour more; check it from time to time, and if it appears dry, top up with extra lamb stock or water.

As the filling slowly cooks, make the hot water pastry (see recipe on page 14) and grease and line the baking tin. After resting the pastry in the fridge, roll it out on a lightly floured surface. In this instance, lining can be done using one large piece of pastry, which could be eased and manipulated into the edges, however, I prefer to assemble the case by making a base, then adhering the sides to it. For more explanation, see the recipe on page 168.

When the tin has been lined, return to the fridge until ready to fill. Any remaining pastry can be used for additional décor.

Remove the lamb from the oven and allow the meat to cool slightly. If the lamb seems a little tough at this point, don't worry, it will have further cooking time within the pastry case. Remove the star anise and rib bones from the lamb and cut the meat into bite-size pieces, drain the sauce into a saucepan (reserving all the other bits), then skim the majority of its fat from the surface and add the cornflour (cornstarch) paste. Bring to the boil to thicken, stirring, then add this to the meat along with the reserved vegetables and other bits. Allow to cool completely.

Continued overleaf

Prepare the potatoes for the topping by cutting into 3mm (⅛in) thick slices, either by hand or using a mandolin. Cut circles from the slices if you want to, and blanch in a pan of boiling, well-salted water for 5 minutes, or until they are almost cooked yet are still holding shape. Drain well. Melt and brown the butter, passing the butter through a fine metal sieve.

Preheat the oven to 180°C (350°F), Gas Mark 4. Fill the pastry case up to three-quarters full with the meat mixture. Top and cover the surface with a layer of potatoes and brush them with the browned butter, sprinkle with salt and pepper, then add another layer of potatoes. Repeat the process, finishing with a neat layer of potatoes on top. Add some pastry décor if you like, brushing this with melted butter, too.

Bake for 1 hour, or until the filling is piping hot and the potatoes fully cooked. Some of the potatoes will crisp and even char in places – this is a good thing. Allow to cool in the tin for 15 minutes, sprinkle the top with thyme leaves, remove from the tin, slice and serve.

This is excellent served with some braised red cabbage.

SAUSAGE AND FIG PLAIT

Agreed, we don't always have the time nor the inclination to make everything from scratch, but if an occasion calls for sausage rolls, say picnic, party or buffet, do try to make these – everyone will remember this sausage roll and you shall be hailed as a domestic hero... possibly.

Unusually, I have used Viennoiserie pastry to encase the sausagemeat here, it works so well and sets this sausage roll aside from the rest.

MAKES 1 LARGE SAUSAGE ROLL,
   TO SERVE 6–12,
   depending on generosity of slice

1 quantity Viennoiserie pastry (see page 26)
plain (all-purpose) flour, for dusting
egg wash (see page 38)

For the filling
50g (1¾oz) smoked pancetta lardons, chopped
70g (2½oz) shallots, very finely chopped
1 fat garlic clove, very finely chopped
20g (scant ¾oz/1 tablespoon) salted butter
Maldon salt and black pepper
sprig of fresh rosemary, leaves removed and finely chopped
½ teaspoon dried oregano
250g (8¾oz) pork mince, the fattier the better
1 teaspoon fennel seeds, toasted and crushed
2 tablespoons chopped parsley
40g (1½oz) dried figs, chopped
handful dried breadcrumbs
1 egg

To finish
aniseed (optional)

ALTERNATIVE & CREATIVE PASTRY

● HW | IP | P | S
○ SH

Prepare the pastry following the recipe on page 26. While the pastry rests in the fridge, make the filling.

Gently dry-fry the pancetta in a pan over a low heat until lightly browned. Remove from the pan with a slotted spoon, leaving any rendered fat in the pan, and place in a large bowl. To the pan, add the chopped shallots, garlic and butter, along with a good pinch of salt. Fry gently until softened, then add the rosemary and oregano, frying for 1 minute more. Add everything to the fried pancetta, then crumble in the minced pork.

Sprinkle in the fennel seeds, parsley, chopped figs and breadcrumbs, stir to combine, then add the egg, mixing everything together. Add a generous grinding of black pepper and stir to combine.

When the dough is ready to be rolled, do so on a lightly floured work surface. Roll to a rectangle approximately 30 x 40cm (12 x 16in) in size, resting occasionally during rolling to prevent springback. Trim off all of the very outer edges. Lay the pastry onto a sheet of baking paper and position so that a shorter edge is facing you. Spoon the sausagemeat mixture down the middle of the rectangle, rounding it off with dampened fingers. Leave a 2cm (¾in) gap both top and bottom, then cut the pastry at each side into equal strips at 2cm (¾in) intervals and at a 45-degree angle. Starting at the top, lift one strip over the meat, then alternate side to

side, crossing the pastry strips over one another, enclosing the filling. Continue until all of the sausagemeat filling has been encased. Secure the ends by sealing and trimming. Slide a baking tray underneath the baking paper and cover loosely with cling film. Leave to prove in a relatively warm place for 1 hour.

Preheat the oven to 180°C (350°F), Gas Mark 4. Carefully and evenly brush the plaited pastry with egg wash, sprinkle with aniseed, if you like, then bake in the oven for 40 minutes or until golden and crisp.

Delicious served hot or cold, and excellent with a good piccalilli.

SLOW-BRAISED PORK CHEEK AND MUSHROOM PIE

Pork has always been my least-favourite meat, and is one I have tried to avoid whenever possible since I was a child. I don't really know why, it's not offensive in flavour nor can I remember having a bad experience with it. What I do remember is my mum trying to fob me off every time she made pork, telling me it was chicken – the obviously porky pork being semi-disguised with sauces of varying descriptions. Because of this hang-up, I would subconsciously flip straight past any pork recipes appearing in cookbooks for years. That is until a Gizzi Erskine recipe tempted me. Gizzi's Pork and Apple Stroganoff with Hot Dog Onions from her book *Slow* made me fall in love with pork for the very first time.

This is an adapted version of that recipe, which happens to work beautifully when encased in crisp hot water pastry.

SERVES 6,
using a specialist oval raised pie mould
measuring 23 x 14 x 8cm (9 x 5½ x 3¼in)

1 quantity Hot Water pastry (see page 14)
butter and plain (all-purpose) flour to
    grease the tin and for rolling
egg wash (see page 38)

For the filling
vegetable oil, for frying
800g (1¾lbs) pork cheeks, each cut into 4,
    tough sinew removed
Maldon salt and black pepper
250g (8¾oz) chestnut mushrooms, cut into
    quarters
250g (8¾oz) button mushrooms, finely
    sliced
250g (8¾oz) white onions, finely sliced
sprig of rosemary, leaves picked and
    chopped
2 Granny Smith apples, peeled, cored and
    each cut into eighths
250ml (8½fl oz/1 cup plus 1 tablespoon)
    dry cider
1 litre (33¾ fl oz/4 cups plus 3 tablespoons)
    pork or chicken stock
2 tablespoons plain (all-purpose) flour
50g (1¾oz) crème fraîche
½ tablespoon mustard, choose your
    favourite
chopped parsley, to taste
juice of ¼ lemon

ALTERNATIVE & CREATIVE PASTRY

● S
○ CH | IP | P | SH | VIE

The meat requires a slow braise, so make the filling first. Heat a large frying pan until hot, then add a little oil. Season the pork cheeks with salt and pepper and fry them in batches until golden brown all over. Remove from the pan and set aside. In the same pan, cook the mushrooms, along with a sprinkling of salt, only adding some more oil if needed. Cook for 20 minutes, during which time the moisture will evaporate and the mushrooms will eventually start to fry, turning golden. Drain on kitchen paper and set aside.

As the mushrooms cook, fry the onions in a separate pan with a splash of oil over a medium heat, until they soften – about 10 minutes. Lower the heat, add some salt, pepper and the rosemary and continue to cook for 15–20 minutes more, until the onions are very soft, melting and golden, then drain on kitchen paper. Add the apple pieces to the hot frying pan – no extra oil is needed – and when golden on all sides, remove from the pan and set aside.

If either of the pans used are big enough, add the pork, mushrooms and onions to it. If not, select a bigger one, but do deglaze any pans previously used with either a splash of cider or stock. Tip in the flour, stir to coat all of the ingredients, then pour in both the cider and stock. Bring the liquid to the boil, and as it does, turn the heat to low and then simmer, uncovered, for

1½ hours, stirring occasionally. Add the apples and continue to simmer for another 30 minutes, checking every so often. The meat should now be meltingly tender. Remove from the heat and allow everything to cool at room temperature within the pan.

While the pie filling is cooling, make the hot water pastry (see recipe and method on page 14). It may be beneficial to grease and flour your pie mould, even if it is non-stick – just in case.

After resting in the fridge, roll the chilled pastry on a lightly floured surface to around 5mm (¼in) thickness. If preferred, one large piece of pastry could be used to line the tin, however, I line mine more like an assemblement of separate pastry pieces. Here's how: using the mould as guide, cut two ovals – one for the base and one for the top. Now cut two long strips each measuring 29 x 8cm (11½ x 3¼in) wide (or to the relevant dimensions of your own tin), these will be the pie walls. Reserve any remaining pastry for decorative flourishes. Chill the cut pastry in the fridge for 30 minutes.

Remove the pastry from the fridge and lay an oval into the base of the mould, pushing the pastry tightly into the sides. Brush the outer edges with egg wash then, using one strip at a time, place along the sides of the mould, adhering the sides to the base, pushing down well to seal. Now push the pastry into and up the side walls of the mould. Repeat with the other side, securing each side to the other – again using the egg wash as a kind of glue. As an extra leakproof precaution, I like to roll a thin strip of pastry to push into all of the seams. Simply adhere the thinly rolled pastry filler with more egg wash and push in place well using a floured finger or utensil. Place back in the fridge until needed. Reserve the egg wash for later.

When the pie filling has cooled, drain off the stock – the liquid needs to be thickened before being added to the pastry case, so return to the pan and gently simmer until reduced by half. Add the crème fraîche and mustard and whisk together. Check for seasoning, add some chopped parsley, to taste, and the lemon juice to balance the richness, then allow to cool fully. Store both meat and sauce separately in the fridge until completely cold.

Add half of the sauce to the meat, then fill the pastry case almost to the top. Using the remaining pastry oval, top the pie and secure the lid to the sides of the pastry case with egg wash, pressing down well to seal. Add some extra décor if wanted, using more egg wash to glue each piece into place. Brush the pie lid with egg wash and pierce a steam hole in the top. Return to the fridge for at least 30 minutes before baking.

Preheat the oven to 180°C (350°F), Gas Mark 4. Bake the pie in the oven for 45 minutes, then carefully remove the pie from its tin, apply more egg wash to the top and brush the sides, before returning to the oven for a further 15–20 minutes to crisp up the sides and until all is beautifully golden and crisp. When fully baked, remove from the oven and rest upon a wire rack. Reheat the reserved sauce to serve alongside.

Serve with some seasonal vegetables. As the pastry is sliced, the juicy filling may ooze out, so be ready to catch the contents. So good.

CRISPY PRAWNS, SWEET AND SOUR

A platter of crispy prawns served alongside a homemade sweet and sour spicy sauce will surely have everyone diving in. Instead of breadcrumbs, I have used dried and crumbled sheet pastry for the coating – the crunchy texture makes a perfect contrast to the succulent prawns.

This is the ideal recipe for using any leftover pieces of stretched sheet pastry.

SERVES 4
as a sharing platter

leftover dried Sheet pastry, or make a full batch (see page 30)
500g (1lb 2oz) raw king prawns, peeled, deveined and tails intact

For the sauce
150ml (5fl oz/⅔ cup) chicken stock
20g (scant ¾oz/1 tablespoon plus 2 teaspoons) palm sugar (or 2 tablespoons caster (superfine) sugar)
2 teaspoons light soy sauce
3 tablespoons Chinese black vinegar, plus extra if liked
3 tablespoons tomato ketchup
juice of ½ lime (optional)
dried chilli flakes (optional and amount to personal taste)
Maldon salt and black pepper
1 tablespoon cornflour (cornstarch), mixed with a little cold water to make a paste

For coating and frying
Maldon salt and black pepper
4 tablespoons plain (all-purpose) flour
1 egg, beaten
500ml (17fl oz/2 cups plus 2 tablespoons) vegetable oil, for deep-frying

To garnish
toasted sesame seeds
spring onions, sliced
red chilli, sliced
coriander leaves and flowers, if available
lime wedges

If you are using leftover sheet pastry, let it dry, uncovered, at room temperature. As it dries, crumble it into small pieces and lay on a tray to crisp further – this should take a couple of hours. When crumbling, you don't need to be precise with the size, varying sizes will add extra texture when fried. If you need to make the pastry, follow the recipe on page 30. Once stretched, allow to dry and crumble as explained. Fully dried, crumbled sheet pastry can be kept in an airtight container and used as an alternative to breadcrumbs.

Make the sauce by adding all of the ingredients, except the cornflour (cornstarch) paste to a saucepan. Bring to a simmer, stirring to dissolve the sugar. Add the cornflour (cornstarch) paste and bring to the boil. When thickened, turn down the heat, simmer for a few more minutes, then taste. Adjust the balance to suit personal taste, add the chilli flakes, if you want some heat, the lime juice, or perhaps more vinegar if you prefer a tangy sauce. Leave in the pan for later.

Tip the pastry crumbs onto a tray or plate and season well with salt and pepper. Season the flour in one bowl, and add the beaten egg to another.

Dry the prawns well on kitchen paper, then coat each in some flour, shaking off any excess. Dip each into the beaten egg and finally roll in the crumbled pastry. Allow to dry for a minute, then roll back through the pastry crumbs, securing plenty of crumbs to the prawns using your fingertips. Lay on kitchen paper until all have been coated.

Heat the oil to 180°C (350°F). Deep-fry the prawns (in small batches if needs be) in a pan of hot oil or deep fat fryer for a couple of minutes. Be sure that the oil is hot enough before frying to ensure that both prawns and pastry cook quickly. Scoop out using a slotted spoon and set on kitchen paper to drain off any excess oil and keep warm until all the prawns have been fried.

Serve the prawns alongside the reheated sauce, sprinkle over the garnishes and squeeze over some lime juice.

SUITABLY KOOKY FISH PIE

I wanted to make a fish pie with a difference, something a little bit kooky – a change from the norm.

There are many variations already, the fillings differing widely, although most are finished with the same soft potato topping. Here I've added baked 'scales' of Gluten-free pastry, which provide texture, some aniseed crunch and, of course, a bit of creative décor. The type of fish used within the pie can be changed to suit personal taste and availability, although the scallops do add a wonderful sweetness, which along with the crunchy pastry and mussel topping, elevate this fish pie to the required level of kooky. This is a very tasty fish pie.

SERVES 4,

using an oval ovenproof dish measuring
22 x 16 x 6cm (8½ x 6¼ x 2½in)

½ quantity Salted Gluten-free pastry (see page 32)
1 teaspoon aniseed, crushed (optional)
cornflour (cornstarch), for dusting

For the mashed potatoes
400g (14oz) King Edward Potatoes, peeled and cut into 5cm (2in) chunks
Maldon salt and white pepper
40g (1½oz/3 tablespoons) unsalted butter, cold, cut into 1cm (½in) cubes
100ml (3½fl oz/⅓ cup plus 1 tablespoon) double (heavy) cream, warmed

For the filling
500ml (17fl oz/2 cups plus 2 tablespoons) fish stock
1 bay leaf
Maldon salt and black pepper
40g (1½oz) leeks, white end only, sliced, washed well
50g (1¾oz) diced onions
1 celery stalk, strings removed, finely diced
60g (2oz) podded broad beans, fresh or frozen
50g (1¾oz) sweetcorn kernels, fresh, canned or frozen
250g (8¾oz) white fish fillet, skinned and cut into 3cm (1¼in) chunks
100g (3½oz) shelled scallops, frozen are fine, thawed weight
small handful of dill, leaves picked
small handful of parsley, finely chopped

For the sauce
150ml (5fl oz/⅔ cup) milk
150ml (5fl oz/⅔ cup) reserved fish stock (from above)
25g (¾oz/1½ tablespoons) salted butter

2 tablespoons cornflour (cornstarch), made into a paste with 1 tablespoon milk
maldon salt and black pepper
fresh nutmeg, for grating (optional)

For the mussel topping
50g (1¾oz) salted butter
1 garlic clove, very finely chopped
juice of ½ lemon
300g (10½oz) fresh mussels, debeard and scrub all and check they are firmly closed
chopped parsley

ALTERNATIVE & CREATIVE PASTRY

● HW | S

Make the pastry following the recipe on page 32, with the addition of the crushed aniseed, if you like. Lightly dust the pastry with cornflour (cornstarch) and roll between two sheets of non-stick baking paper to around 3mm (⅛in) depth. Place in the freezer for 15 minutes.

In the meantime, prepare the mash. Place the potatoes in a pan of cold well-salted water and bring to the boil, then boil for 12–15 minutes or until the potatoes are tender. Drain and allow to steam-dry for 1 minute. Mash the potatoes until lump-free. Return to the pan, add the butter and cream, a little at a time, beating well until it has all been added. Check the seasoning and, if needed, add some more salt, along with a good pinch of white pepper. Leave in the pan, covering with a layer of cling film until later.

Preheat the oven to 180°C (350°F), Gas Mark 4. Remove the pastry from the freezer and cut out as many discs as possible using a 3cm (1¼in) round pastry cutter, then cut each in half. Lay these on a baking tray lined with non-stick baking paper and bake in the oven for up to 15 minutes, removing when crisp and golden. Cool on a wire rack and save for later.

To cook the vegetables, heat the fish stock in a large saucepan and add the bay leaf and some salt and pepper. Bring to boil then add the leeks, onions and celery. Reduce the heat and simmer for 5 minutes. Add the broad beans and sweetcorn (only if using fresh) and simmer for 1 minute more. Remove all the veg with a slotted spoon and drain on a clean, dry cloth. I prefer to remove the tough skins from the broad beans, so do so, too, if you wish. Keep the stock simmering.

Add the white fish fillet chunks to the stock, bring to the boil, then immediately remove from the heat. Allow the fish to sit in the hot stock for 4 minutes only, after which time, remove using a slotted spoon and drain well. Pass the stock through a sieve, measuring out 150ml (5fl oz). Reserve the remainder for cooking the mussels with later. Add the milk to the jug of measured stock for the sauce, making 300ml (10fl oz/1¼ cups) of liquid.

Continued overleaf

Make a white sauce by melting the butter in a clean saucepan. Add the milky stock to the pan and bring to the boil. Pour in the cornflour (cornstarch) paste and whisk well. Return to the boil to thicken, whisking, then simmer for a few minutes. Season well, adding some nutmeg if desired. Allow to cool.

Preheat the oven to 160°C (325°F), Gas Mark 3. To the ovenproof dish, add the vegetables, cooked white fish, scallops, herbs and some salt and pepper. Stir well, then add the white sauce and combine. Top with the mashed potato (which may need loosening with some milk), then top that with the pastry scales. Cover with kitchen foil and bake in the oven for 30 minutes, then remove the foil and bake for a further 10 minutes.

During those final 10 minutes, prepare everything for the mussel topping. Heat a small frying pan and add the butter. Allow the butter to froth, then add the garlic. Cook for 1 minute, swirling the pan continuously to prevent burning, then squeeze in the lemon juice and remove from the heat.

Set an empty saucepan over a high heat. When super hot, tip in the mussels and a good splash of the remaining fish stock. Cover with a lid and allow the mussels to cook for 3–4 minutes, shaking the pan from time to time, until all of the shells have opened (discard any that remain closed). Drain through a colander, pick the mussels from their shells, and toss into the garlicky butter. Reheat this ever so slightly, add some chopped parsley and then top the pie with the garlicky mussels.

Serve with a green salad. I have used a selection of ice plant, oxalis, houttuynia, and dill fronds and flowers.

CRAB AND FENNEL VOL-AU-VENTS

Are vol-au-vents a bit retro? Probably, but I still love them and I'm sure everyone else does, too. When made using homemade puff pastry they are as light as air – a perfect little receptacle to which you can add anything sweet or savoury. Here I have made medium-sized vol-au-vents, just large enough to serve as a starter, a light lunch or supper. If preferred, you can make smaller, party-size vol-au-vents instead, just change the cutter size – the method will remain the same.

MAKES 6 MEDIUM-SIZE VOL-AU-VENTS

1 quantity Puff pastry (see page 16)
egg wash (see page 38)

For the filling
60g (2oz) fennel bulb, shaved very finely
juice of 1 small lemon
Maldon salt and black pepper
1 mild red chilli, deseeded and finely
    chopped (optional)
fresh dill, leaves picked
100g (3½oz) picked white crab meat
150g (5⅓oz) best-quality cooked and peeled
    prawns
6 teaspoons Fennel Jam (see page 90)
    (optional)

For the sauce
1 tablespoon mayonnaise, homemade or
    shop-bought
1½ tablespoons tomato ketchup
salt and pinch of cayenne pepper
6 drops of Worcestershire sauce
juice of ½ lemon
Maldon salt and black pepper

To garnish
citrusy leaves, such as oxalis and tagete
    (optional)
edible flowers, borage work well (optional)
reserved fennel fronds
extra virgin olive oil
black pepper

ALTERNATIVE & CREATIVE PASTRY

● IP | VIE
○ CH | GF | HW | S | SH

Make the pastry following the recipe on page 16. After the final resting, roll out to a 5mm (¼in) thickness.

When the pastry has been rolled, rest in the fridge for at least 30 minutes, after which cut out 12 squares using an 8cm (3¼in) pastry cutter. Lay six of the squares on a baking tray lined with non-stick baking paper, leaving enough room between each for expansion during baking. Brush the surface of each vol-au-vent with egg wash, being careful not to let any drip down the sides of the pastry.

Cut a 5cm (2in) circle in the centre of the remaining six squares, but leave the circle in place. Stack these squares (circle intact) on top of the egg-washed squares, keeping all sides in line as best as you can.

Preheat the oven to 180°C (350°F), Gas Mark 4. Brush the top of each vol-au-vent with the remaining egg wash, again being careful not to let any drip down the sides (this, too, can affect the rise during baking). Another good tip for an even rise is to set an ovenproof food ring or, in this case, square mould over the top of each vol-au-vent, which will support the rise; however, freestanding vol-au-vents can be made successfully as the ones pictured were. Either way, bake in the oven for 25 minutes, after which time, cut out the central circular piece (and discard), push down the middle part of the pastry and return to the oven for a further 10 minutes or so, until all are crisp and golden. Allow to cool on a wire rack.

To prepare the filling, place the shaved fennel in a bowl with the lemon juice, some salt, a little pepper, the chopped chilli and dill. Fork through the crab meat and add this to the fennel along with the prawns. Check for seasoning, adjusting if needs be.

Make the sauce by mixing everything together with a little seasoning and add as much as desired to the seafood and fennel. Any extra sauce could be served separately for those that prefer more.

To assemble, add a teaspoon of the fennel jam (if using) to the bottom of each pastry case. Top with the seafood mixture and garnish with a small arrangement of leaves, edible flowers and herbs (if using). Drizzle with olive oil and a generous grinding of pepper and serve as they are.

*Vol-au-vents can be unpredictable during baking, mostly because they may rise more on one side due to uneven rolling, even if that is only very slight. The secret to achieving consistent, evenly risen vol-au-vents is to roll the pastry to the same thickness throughout, to do this, roll strips of pastry through a pasta machine prior to cutting, with the roller on the widest setting. The pastry does have to be chilled yet pliable to do this, so as not to disrupt the buttery layers created during the folding process – so please do this with caution, or even leave out this stage if you're not too fussed about a wonky vol-au-vent. They will, of course, taste the same!

COD AND SALSA WITH PUFF PASTRY TACOS

Mexican food has such explosion of flavour on the palate – fresh, vibrant, zingy and spicy. It rates highly among my favourite cuisines of the world. I've replaced the traditional corn tacos with puff pastry ones – quirky, yes; delicious, definitely.

SERVES 4

1 quantity Puff pastry (see page 16)
plain (all-purpose) flour, for dusting
egg wash (see page 38)

For the salsa

3 ripe but firm salad tomatoes, skin and
 seeds removed, finely chopped
1 small garlic clove, very finely chopped
½ red onion, very finely sliced
juice of 1 lime
¼ teaspoon ground cumin
¼ teaspoon dried chipotle chilli flakes
2 tablespoons roughly chopped coriander
 leaves
1 teaspoon finely chopped mint leaves
1 teaspoon Maldon salt

For the cod

2 tablespoons plain (all-purpose) flour
½ teaspoon chilli powder
½ teaspoon ground cumin
¼ teaspoon fine salt
500g (18oz) cod loin or fillet, skinned and
 cut into 3cm (1¼in) pieces
oil, for frying

To finish (all optional)

spring onions, finely sliced
coriander leaves and flowers (optional)
extra chilli

ALTERNATIVE & CREATIVE PASTRY

● IP | VIE

Make the pastry following the recipe on page 16, up to and including the final resting. If the pastry has been made in advance, see notes on page 38 prior to rolling.

Roll out on a lightly floured work surface to 5mm (¼in) thick, trim off the very outer edges and allow to relax on the work surface for at least 5 minutes. Using an 8cm (3¼in) circular cutter, cut out as many rounds from the rolled pastry as possible. Using the same cutter, cut a section from the bottom of each, creating a fat, crescent-like shape. Spread across a baking tray lined with non-stick baking paper, leaving a sufficient gap between each to allow for expansion. Return to the fridge for 30 minutes.

Preheat the oven to 180°C (350°F), Gas Mark 4. Retrieve the pastry from the fridge and, using the back of a knife, score each piece with a decorative criss-cross pattern. Brush the surface of each 'taco' with the egg wash and then bake in the oven for 25 minutes, after which time they should be crisp and golden. Remove from the oven and allow to cool on a wire rack, then arrange on a serving platter.

To make the salsa, mix the chopped tomatoes with all of the other ingredients in a serving bowl, adjusting the flavours to suit personal taste.

Prepare the cod. Mix together the flour, ground spices and salt in a bowl, then roll the pieces of cod through it, shaking off the excess. Transfer to a plate.

Heat a large, non-stick frying pan over a medium heat and add a splash of oil. Fry the fish for a few minutes until just cooked, carefully turning the fish with a palette knife. When done, transfer to a serving plate and take all of the components to the table.

To serve, break into the centre of a 'taco' shell, add some fish, top with some salsa, then sprinkle over some spring onions, adding a little more coriander and chilli, if you like.

A chilled Mexican beer would be my choice of drink to wash down these delicious 'tacos'!

CHAPTER 7

Crunch & Crumb

STRUDEL SCRUNCHES

Myles, my youngest son, is my trusted critic when it comes to anything pastry. At the grand age of 6, he can tell me when something is amiss, or in this case, when something is perfect. He deemed these strudel scrunches to be his favourite of all the pastries I have ever made and, based on his verdict, I am confident that these will be a winner in your home, too.

If you are making a scrunch topping for a savoury pie, omit the sugar and replace it with salt and black pepper or another seasoning that will complement the dish.

MAKES 1–6,
depending on size required

1 quantity Sheet pastry (see page 30)
60g (2¼oz/¼ cup) unsalted butter, melted
100g (3½oz/½ cup) caster (superfine) sugar

Make the pastry following the recipe on page 30. After resting, stretch the pastry (see tips and techniques on page 30) and cut into squares relevant to the size of scrunch required. Allow to dry on the table or work surface it has been stretched over.

Use the melted butter to brush the surface of each cut square and sprinkle evenly with sugar. Leave to dry for up to 3 hours (depending on the environment) before shaping. The pastry needs to be stiff enough to hold some shape, yet still pliable enough to manipulate into the moulds without breaking.

If making small scrunches, set them in a muffin tray, if making one large scrunch, to top a pie (see page 158), say, set into an appropriately sized loose-bottomed tart tin. When the strudel squares are semi-dry, ease and fold them into each mould, the folds and edges will create height and texture. Use at least two squares per small scrunch, more for larger ones. Allow to dry further, at room temperature, for at least 4 hours or, even better, overnight.

Preheat the oven to 180°C (350°F), Gas Mark 4. Bake the scrunches for 5 minutes before taking a look – they will cook and colour quickly due to how fine and dry the pastry is already. However, a few more minutes may be required to achieve a lovely golden hue – just be vigilant after the 5-minute point. When done, remove from their moulds and set on a wire rack to cool.

These are best eaten minutes after they've come out of the oven, as soon as they have cooled sufficiently. Utterly delicious on their own, or perhaps pair with some poached fruit, as on page 50.

MINI BEIGNETS

These mini beignets are a perfect way to use up any leftover choux pastry. A surprising amount can be made from very little batter, due to the little balls puffing up as they fry. They are lovely simply rolled in sugar, or you can add some extra flavourings, such as aromatic spices or citrus zest. Here I have used aniseed and chamomile – a fresh and moreish combination.

MAKES PLENTY!

200g (7oz) Choux pastry (see page 24)

For frying and finishing
500ml (18fl oz/2 cups plus 2 tablespoons) vegetable oil
150g (5¼oz/¾ cup) caster (superfine) sugar
1 chamomile tea bag, contents emptied
1 teaspoon toasted aniseed

If using leftover choux pastry, simply transfer to a piping bag fitted with a 1cm (½in) plain nozzle. If the choux pastry needs to be made, follow the recipe on page 24. Leave the pastry at room temperature.

Preheat the oil to 180°C (350°F) in either a deep-fat fryer or a suitable pan. Spread the sugar over a large plate or tray. Mix through the dried chamomile from the tea bag, along with the toasted seeds, distributing evenly.

Have a sharp knife nearby. In one hand, hold the piping bag above and as close to the hot oil as is safe to do. Gently squeeze the bag until the choux appears from the nozzle. Dip the tip of the knife into the hot oil and use it to cut the stream of paste at 1cm (½in) intervals. I suggest frying in batches, moving the little balls around in the oil so they colour evenly. When done, lift out using a slotted spoon and drain on

kitchen paper. When still hot, roll in the flavoured sugar, then leave to cool (at least a little) before eating.

CROISSANT CUBES

When I first saw Bedros Kabranian's croissant cube on Instagram, I knew I wouldn't settle until I had worked out how it was made. It was obvious that it was baked in a specialist mould, probably under weight, but the folding and the interior of the cubes had my mind a-boggle. Each and every one made by Bedros is perfect, the folds exact, the edges super sharp. Where mine are nowhere near as perfect as his, I have managed to achieve a decent cube, and all from using the leftover scraps of pastry from the recipes on pages 56 and 102.

There are countless options and shapes in which to bake viennoiserie. Click on the explore function on Instagram and hashtag #viennoiserie, make a full batch of dough (see page 26) and get experimenting!

MAKES 2 CUBES,
using two 6.5cm (2½in) square food
moulds

leftover Viennoiserie dough from either
pages 56 or 102

After cutting the squares from the pastry as instructed on either of the individual recipes, a pastry trellis (of sorts) will be left behind. This is what will be used to make the cubes.

Set the moulds on top of a baking tray lined with non-stick baking paper. Cut the pastry 'trellis' diagonally into four pieces. Roll up, as best as possible, and lay two rolled pieces into each mould, altering the angles to which they are laid. It may seem a bit of a tangle but as the dough proves, it will fill out into the sides of the moulds and the gaps will be filled. Cover loosely with cling film and leave in a relatively warm place to prove for up to 3 hours (see the timeline and notes on proving on page 28).

Preheat the oven to 180°C (350°F), Gas Mark 4. When the dough has almost reached the top of the moulds, place in the oven, lay a baking sheet over the top and weigh that down with an ovenproof pot or some baking tins. Bake under the weight for 20 minutes before lifting off the weight and removing the

moulds. The cubes should be cooked through after this time, however, if a few more minutes are needed for extra colour, return to the oven without the moulds and bake until dark golden.

Cool on wire racks before serving.

ARLETTES

When working out whether or not to include inverted puff pastry in this book, I made a batch and used it solely to make Arlettes. The debate was over from the first bite – the answer was a 100 per cent yes. These wafer-thin morsels are hands down the most delicate, flavoursome, crisp and utterly divine biscuits that I have ever tasted. Don't doubt it, make the inverted puff pastry, make these biscuits, and I'm sure you will agree. They are a total joy to eat. They can also be used as wafers which work beautifully when used to sandwich ice cream.

MAKES 25 BISCUITS

1 quantity Inverted Puff pastry (see page 20)
flour, for dusting

For filling and finishing
50g (1¾oz/¼ cup) caster (superfine) sugar
2 teaspoons ground cinnamon
200g (7oz/1½ cups minus 1 tablespoon)
   icing (powdered) sugar, sifted

ALTERNATIVE & CREATIVE PASTRY

● P

Make the inverted puff pastry following the recipe on page 20. After the final fold, rest the pastry in the fridge for 1 hour. If the pastry has been made further in advance, see notes on page 19 before rolling.

Lightly dust both sides of the pastry with flour and roll the dough in between two sheets of non-stick baking paper to a rectangle measuring approximately 40 x 30cm (16 x 12in). Trim off the very outer edges, reserving the scraps.

Mix together the sugar and cinnamon and use to evenly cover the surface of the pastry. Starting at a shorter end, roll the pastry into a long log, not too tightly – the layers do need some space to expand during baking. Wrap the pastry log in cling film and chill in the fridge for 1 hour.

After chilling, trim each end to neaten, then slice the remainder into 1cm (½in) rounds. As before, keep any trimmed pastry to bake and eat as scraps.

Lay a sheet of non-stick baking paper on the worktop and pile up the icing (powdered) sugar. Dip each slice into the icing sugar, coating both sides well. Flatten each with a rolling pin using an upwards motion, creating an oval. If wanting to be neat, you could use an oval cutter, but it's not essential.

Before baking the whole batch, I suggest baking one biscuit first. The process of making Arlettes, although very much

worthwhile, is quite laborious and time-consuming. I shudder to imagine a whole batch being baked only to burn due to oven fluctuation. It does happen – not only do ovens vary from one manufacturer to the next, the metal used to make baking trays does, too – as will the depth to which each baker will roll their biscuits… there's a lot to consider! Bake one, using my timings and method below as a starting point. Then when you are happy with the baking time needed, go ahead and bake the rest. The baking stage may need to be done in batches, depending on how many baking trays are available.

Preheat the oven to 180°C (350°F), Gas Mark 4. Line a baking tray with non-stick baking paper and lay the Arlettes in rows, leaving a good gap between each to allow for expansion. Top with another sheet of baking paper and then top that with another baking tray. Bake under weight for 12 minutes. When fully baked the Arlettes will be crisp and golden brown.

Remove from the tray using a palette knife and cool on a wire rack. As the wafers cool the caramelized icing (powdered) sugar will harden, creating a caramel crunch like no other.

Store in an airtight container – best eaten within 2 days.

RASPBERRY STRAWS

A party food classic, puff pastry straws will always have everyone reaching for the bundle. The expected and unsurprising cheese versions are, of course, delicious, but these tangy raspberry straws are a real treat, and even though sweet, they would make a novel addition to a cheese board.

These straws can be successfully prepared and frozen unbaked (as pictured), then baked fresh when needed.

MAKES 15–20 STRAWS

1 quantity Puff pastry (see page 16)

For the jam
250g (8¾oz) raspberries, fresh or frozen – if frozen, defrost before use
60g (2oz/5 tablespoons) caster (superfine) sugar
juice of ¼ lemon
pinch of salt

ALTERNATIVE & CREATIVE PASTRY

● P

Make the pastry following the recipe on page 16. After the final fold and once rested, roll out to approximately 30 x 30cm (12 x 12in) and trim off the very outer edges. Place in the fridge until needed. If the pastry has been made further in advance, see the note on page 19.

To make the jam, squash the raspberries with the back of a spoon, then transfer to a small saucepan with all the other jam ingredients. Gently simmer until the sugar dissolves, then increase the heat for a couple of minutes. When the mixture starts to thicken, reduce the heat to a slow simmer and cook for 10–12 minutes – the juices will turn jam-like, coating the back of a spoon easily. When done, transfer to a bowl and allow to cool completely.

Collect the pastry from the fridge and cut the square in half. Spread a layer of cooled jam across the surface of one piece and lay the other piece of pastry directly on top – any extra jam can be stored in a screw-top jar in the fridge for up to 3 weeks.

Cut the pastry sandwich into strips approximately 1cm (½in) wide. Twist each pastry strip, turning the ends in opposite directions to create a rope effect, showing the red jammy centre between the turns. Line a baking tray with non-stick baking paper, then lay the straws on top, leaving plenty of room between each one to allow for expansion during baking.

Preheat the oven to 180°C (350°F), Gas Mark 4. Bake the straws in the oven for 15 minutes until crisp and golden. If, like me, you prefer tighter, crunchier straws, remove from the oven after 8 minutes, and while still soft, carefully (they'll be hot!) re-twist to tighten. Finish baking, then cool on wire racks before eating.

TEAR AND DUNK VIENNOISERIE LOAF

I find the layering in viennoiserie beautiful to eat. Crisp and crunchy on the outside, soft and chewy on the inside. This is such a treat when eaten fresh still hot from the oven and, as discovered by my boys, it's heavenly when dunked into a chocolate caramel spread!

MAKES 1 LOAF,
depending on size and shape

1 quantity Viennoiserie pastry (see page 26)
flour, for dusting
egg wash (see page 38)

Make the dough following the recipe on page 26. After the final fold and resting in the fridge, roll out on a lightly floured work surface to a thickness of 5mm (¼in), trying to keep it in a rectangular shape. It is important to allow the pastry to rest occasionally during rolling, to prevent it from springing back. When rolled, place in the freezer for 5 minutes. Trim all of the outer edges to neaten, a pizza wheel will do this job perfectly.

Roll up starting at one of the longest sides, not too tightly, into a log. With sharp scissors, snip into the top of the dough at 4cm (1½in) intervals, snipping almost but not quite all the way through the roll. Position each cut piece either left or right of centre, alternating the direction with each piece. Cover loosely with cling film and leave to prove in a relatively warm place for up to 3 hours. (See notes on page 28.)

Preheat the oven to 180°C (350°F), Gas Mark 4. Place the loaf on a baking tray lined with non-stick baking paper and brush the smooth surfaces with egg wash, avoiding the cut-through layers, as this will affect the rise and separation of them during baking. Bake the loaf in the oven for 35 minutes, or until crisp and dark golden. If the top is colouring a little too much before the end of the baking time, simply cover with some kitchen foil.

Remove from the oven and allow to cool slightly before tearing, sharing and dunking!

SEEDED CRACKERS

Don't waste any stretched sheet pastry, after all, the process requires plenty of effort. To discard even the smallest piece would seem a great shame. If any should be left over from a recipe, brush with melted butter, layer up, sprinkle with seeds and bake into crackers. Simple, but very effective.

The recipe below is for making a full batch of crackers.

MAKES 10–25,
depending on size and shape

1 quantity Sheet pastry (see page 30)

For the butter and seasonings
80g (2¾oz) melted butter
150g (5½oz) mixed seeds
wild garlic salt (see suppliers, page 202)
cracked black pepper
dried edible flowers (see suppliers, page 202)

Make and stretch the pastry following the recipe on page 30. Allow to dry a little then brush the entire surface with melted butter.

Sprinkle the pastry with a mixture of the seeds, wild garlic salt, pepper and dried flowers, then cut into squares – any size, depending on personal preference. If making the size as shown opposite, first cut the pastry into 20cm (8in) squares.

Fold each square in half vertically, enveloping the seasonings, then fold again in the same manner. Neaten the outer edges with a pizza wheel, then cut in half lengthways. Transfer to a baking sheet lined with non-stick baking paper and repeat with the remaining squares.

Brush each cracker with a little more of the melted butter and add some more seasonings. Allow to dry for an hour.

Preheat the oven to 180°C (350°F), Gas Mark 4. Bake the crackers for 8–10 minutes until crisp and golden. Transfer to a wire rack to cool.

These crackers are best eaten on the day they are made.

Mallow

Nigella (for seeds)

Rose

Viola

Forget-me-not

Rocket

Mimulus

Thyme

Houttuynia

SUPPLIERS

UK

Silverwood Bakeware –for a wide selection of all bakeware needs
www.silverwood-bakeware.com

Maddocks Farm – for a vast selection of beautiful organic edible
flowers and leaves, wild garlic salt and dried flower petals
www.maddocksfarmorganics.co.uk

La Fromagerie – a dream haven for cheese and food lovers
www.lafromagerie.co.uk

Peter Tyson – stockist of kitchen equipment and appliances
www.petertysonappliances.co.uk

Saunders Chocolates – for artisan chocolate or éclair toppers
www.saunderschocolates.co.uk

Divertimenti – a wonderful one stop shop for cooking enthusiasts
www.divertimenti.co.uk

KitchenAid – get one if you can, you will not regret it
www.kitchenaid.co.uk

US & AUS

Food52 – endless temptation on all things food-related
www.food52.com

Chef's Hat – all the essentials for both home cooks and professionals
www.chefshat.com.au

Essential Ingredient – quality ingredients, cookware and
everything needed to inspire better cooking
www.essentialingredient.com.au

EQUIPMENT

Free-standing mixer: My KitchenAid, although my most expensive piece of kitchen equipment, is also my most used. I simply love it and I do recommend investing in one if you can. Ten years down the line, mine is still as good as new and I envisage that it will be for a life-time.

Bakeware: I have a wide selection of bakeware, primarily made by Silverwood. The quality and consistency of finish their products bring to my baking is unquestionable. They will last a lifetime if cared for properly and will undoubtedly help to achieve the desired results. I would recommend investing at the very least in a Tatin Dish, two sizes and shapes of Loose-bottomed Tart Tins, two medium-sized baking trays (essential for baking puff pastry between) and the Simple Simon pie tin, an absolute favourite of mine. You may find it hard not to buy the whole range!

Mixing bowls of all sizes are often used in my kitchen. I love the ones with measurements and a pouring spout.

Knives: I have a beautiful Japanese knife that I take great pleasure in using every day. It was expensive but it, without doubt, makes my prep more efficient. I mostly use the same knife for every job, but some prefer a smaller one for smaller items, or certain knives for specific jobs. Whatever your preference – keep them sharp, it makes all the difference. As well as sharp knives – palette knives are indispensable utensils, both straight and cranked, large and small.

Mandolin: I use a Zyliss Swiss mandolin for preparing the apples for the Apple Rose Tart, and have found this the absolute best mandolin for the job. It has many other attachments, too should you need them.

Peeler: A Swiss-style swivel-headed vegetable peeler is the best tool to use for shaving pastry cases.

Pastry Brushes: As well as a standard pastry brush, I use a variety of artist and make-up brushes for use when egg-washing pastry tops. The smaller brushes will aid with an even brushing and won't dislodge any carefully placed pastry décor.

Oven thermometer: Essential, unless you really know your oven. The difference between the dial to that of the actual oven temperature can be quite surprising.

Rolling pin: A pin that feels right under hand is what works best. I have three pins of varying sizes and material, yet I only tend to use one which is old and wooden – the most basic of them all.

Decorative cutters: I use the plunger type, those used for cutting fondant icing for cakes. They cut and emboss pastry beautifully.

Non-stick baking paper: The white silicone-coated paper would be my choice, but if the brown greaseproof paper is all that you can find please be aware that it may stick and isn't suitable for pouring hot caramel onto.

Pasta machine: A great piece of kit for rolling and cutting pastry for certain jobs. I have an Imperia Classic, which is great. It is solid and feels sturdy during rolling. Do remember never to wash your machine as the water gets trapped between the rollers and the metal rusts. Instead, just let any crumbs that get lodged in between the rollers air-dry, they will crumble and fall out on the next use. If you have a KitchenAid, the pasta rolling attachments work equally as well.

INDEX

fines 106

pecans: chocolate, pecan and Brazil nut bars 124

frangipane, persimmon and grape tart 109–11

pies: boozy cherry liquor pie 62
  chicken, chorizo and spinach pie 155–7
  chocolate, cherry and almond pithiviers 122
  decorating 42
  gluten-free lemon meringue pie 73–5
  my Mum's 'tatty pot' (pie) 161–5
  oxtail scrunch pot pie 158–60
  slow-braised pork cheek and mushroom pie 168–71
  suitably kooky fish pie 176–8
  tartiflette pies 85
  trinary pie 132

pine nuts: pine nut praline, rum and raisin pinwheels 102
  spinach 'figura di otto' 147

pinwheels, pine nut praline, rum and raisin 102

pistachio tart with rhubarb tiles 118–21

pithiviers, chocolate, cherry and almond 122

pork: sausage and fig plait 166
  slow-braised pork cheek and mushroom pie 168–71

potatoes: leek, potato and Cheddar cheese cubes 143–5
  my Mum's 'tatty pot' (pie) 161–5
  peanut and potato satay bites 117
  suitably kooky fish pie 176–8
  tartiflette pies 85

praline: Paris Brest with cherries and dipped hazelnuts 112–15
  pine nut praline, rum and raisin pinwheels 102

prawns: crab and fennel vol-au-vents 179–81
  crispy prawns, sweet and sour 172

puff pastry 16–19
  apple tarte tatin 59
  arlettes 192
  beetroot tarte tatin 150
  chocolate, cherry and almond pithiviers 122

crab and fennel vol-au-vents 179–81
inverted puff pastry 20–3
cod and salsa with puff pastry tacos 182
raspberry and rose gin mille feuille 70–2
  raspberry straws 194
  salted caramel banana tarte tatins 65
  vanilla slices 83
  vegetable patch(work) tart 128
  vegetable Wellington 148

R

raisins: pine nut praline, rum and raisin pinwheels 102

raspberries: raspberry and rose gin mille feuille 70–2
  raspberry coulis 50
  raspberry straws 194
  roasted rhubarb and raspberry tart 48

resting pastry 38

rhubarb: pistachio tart with rhubarb tiles 118–21
  roasted rhubarb and raspberry tart 48

rice: peanut and potato satay bites 117

ricotta cheese: pastiera Napoletana 98

rolling pastry 36–8

rose garden effect decoration 42

rosemary, crystallized 80

rotolo, chestnut and mushroom 131

rum: pine nut praline, rum and raisin pinwheels 102

S

salad leaves: celeriac and apple tarte fin 140

salsa: cod and salsa with puff pastry tacos 182

salted & sweet vegan pastry 34–5

salted caramel banana tarte tatins 65

salted gluten-free pastry 32–3
  celeriac and apple tarte fin 140
  onion and egg tartlets 134
  suitably kooky fish pie 176–8
  walnut, pear and Regalis tarte fines 106

salted shortcrust pastry 10–11
  chicken, chorizo and spinach pie 155–7

goat's cheese and fennel jam galette 90

super slow onion and Gruyère tart 94

trinary pie 132

satay: peanut and potato satay bites 117

sausage and fig plait 166

scallops: suitably kooky fish pie 176–8

seafood: crab and fennel vol-au-vents 179–81
  crispy prawns, sweet and sour 172
  suitably kooky fish pie 176–8

seeded crackers 198

shallots: trinary pie 132

sheet pastry 30–1
  butterscotch crunch with crystallized rosemary 80
  chestnut and mushroom rotolo 131
  crispy prawns, sweet and sour 172
  oxtail scrunch pot pie 158–60
  peanut and potato satay bites 117
  poached peach, zabaglione and sweet strudel scrunch 50
  seeded crackers 198
  spinach 'figura di otto' 147
  griddled greens, cauliflower and lemon triangles 138
  strudel scrunches 187

shortcrust pastry: salted shortcrust pastry 10–11
  sweet shortcrust pastry 12–13

shrinkage, preventing 38

spinach: chicken, chorizo and spinach pie 155–7
  spinach 'figura di otto' 147

spiral effect decoration 42

griddled greens, cauliflower and lemon triangles 138

strudel: poached peach, zabaglione and sweet strudel scrunch 50
  strudel scrunches 187

suitably kooky fish pie 176–8

sultanas: spinach 'figura di otto' 147

super slow onion and Gruyère tart 94

sweet gluten-free pastry 32–3
  gluten-free lemon meringue pie 73–5

sweet shortcrust pastry 12–13
  apple rose tart (2020) 53–5
  boozy cherry liquor pie 62
  chamomile panna cotta tart 78
  chocolate, pecan and Brazil nut bars

ACKNOWLEDGEMENTS

I have thoroughly enjoyed every moment spent writing this book, and subsequently writing these thank yous. Reflecting back on the whole experience, appreciating the passion and dedication that the rest of the team has offered has been heart-warming. It is, after all, the accumulated help, support and dedication of many that brings a book to life. I feel blessed to have had so much encouragement along the way, with the opportunity to work alongside a true band of amazing individuals, starting with those at Kyle books.

Jo, thank you so much for giving me the opportunity to write this book, it is only as special as it is because you believed that I could do it, I thoroughly enjoy working with you and hope we can go on to make many more books together. Issy, special thanks to you for being a fun, understanding and meticulous editor. For listening to and answering all of my random messages and brain storming. We really did make a stunning book, thank you. Of course, my gratitude expands to the wider team at Kyle Books and Octopus, who work away in the background to make every single book special.

Rachel, your calming presence always makes shoot days composed days. Thank you so much for the beautiful design and help in selecting the right props for the photographs. Your chic serenity is evident on every page. I love it and love working with you. Cynthia, thank you too for selecting such a considered gathering of props to choose from. Pete, I very much enjoyed working with you. I have spent many hours looking over the images, wowed by how you have captured my recipes. I shall always consider the Rose Gin Jelly a favourite, not only for its beauty, but because I believe after that shot we understood each other. Thank you for your patience, for understanding me, and for bearing my slightly eccentric behaviour!

Heather, my lovely agent, thank you for representing me. From the very second that we met, I knew you were the agent for me. Your direct approach, honesty, and enthusiasm is everything. I love it.

Andy (Mr Stacey); always an unwavering pillar of support. There is no way on this Earth that I could have got through all of that prep without you, you are a true friend and knight in shining armour. I often wonder how you put up with me and my kitchen idiosyncrasies... I can only fathom that you are indeed a saint. Bless you.

To my friends, my 'chef de plunges', you know I use that phrase with great affection and humour. Bev, Issa, Pauline, Sam, Sandra, Tanya, Vicki and Cara, I am the luckiest girl to have friends and a niece like you. Thank you so much for being a part of the process and making prep days and shoot days such fun days. Having you there meant those hours were stress-free, which undoubtedly has been reflected in the book... a book that would never have been in the first place, if my new found friend, Mandy, hadn't introduced me to Jo. The power of friendship is a very powerful thing indeed! I love you all.

Special thanks to Abi, even though heavily pregnant you came to help me during the first shoot. It's safe to say that we had a giggle and I'm sure we will always think of Oscar's burning question when we reminisce about our time together – what an absolute hoot. Thank you so much for your incredible touch, I really enjoyed having you on board.

Jamie Oliver, one of the kindest and most encouraging people in the business. The support that you offer me is just incredible. Thank you so much for the use of the studio for the latter part of photography, it really did make those shots extra special. You inspire me so much - in turn I hope I do you proud.

Love and thanks to Silverwood Bakeware, who without the use of their amazing wares I would not have been able to produce the variety and quality of dishes that I was able to. I will be forever grateful for your cooperation with this project and I hope that our relationship will continue for many years to come. To PJ and the team at Peter Tyson Carlisle, for sending the gorgeous pistachio KitchenAid to my London shoot.

My wonderful family, each and every one of you help to keep me motivated and rally around me in so many different ways, I don't know what I'd do without you, I love you all. My beautiful boys, Evan, Oscar and Myles, you are everything to me. Thank you for being you, all so different, all so special. Jonah, thank you for being both Mum & Dad to our boys during the final stages of the book, I really couldn't have given it my absolute all otherwise.

A lifetime of gratitude goes to my lovely Mum. She instilled in me from a young age that 'if a job was worth doing, it was worth doing well'. I hope with this book I have done just that, and all of my Mum's influences shine through. I truly believe they do.

Finally, I thank you the reader and loyal Instagram follower, for both buying this book and engaging with my posts online. Without you, this book would never have been made. I hope with all my heart that you will love it as much as I do.